Changing Your Mindset for Good

The Quick Way to Control Your Emotions, Shift Your Reality for Mental Self Development

Jay Fenix

within this book has been derived from various sources. Please consult a licensed professional before attempting any techniques outlined in this book.

By reading this document, the reader agrees that under no circumstances is the author responsible for any losses, direct or indirect, that are incurred as a result of the use of the information contained within this document, including, but not limited to, errors, omissions, or inaccuracies.

ISBN : 978-1-3999-3421-3

Contents

Introduction

Control your thoughts. Decide about that which you will think and concentrate upon. You are in charge of your life to the degree you take charge of your thoughts.

—Earl Nightingale

I've heard that when an author decides to put pen and paper together and write a book, it's usually for two good reasons. The first is that the author is an expert on the subject. The second is that they feel passionately about an issue or problem that others in society are also facing, and want to provide answers to their questions, in which they are sure others have been asking the same exact questions internally. In this case, the latter makes more sense, and I'll explain why.

I want to ask you a simple question to begin with: Have you ever had a really bad day? One of those days where you just felt extremely frustrated, and you felt as if nothing went right? Maybe you got up late for work or school, your car refused to start, or perhaps you got into an extremely heated argument with a close friend that left you feeling pretty much blue. I have had a lot of those days, where I felt as if my life was a mess. I've felt overwhelmed and as if I was no longer in control, and I'm pretty sure you've had those days too. I asked that question because I want you to dig a little deeper; can you think of anything that you could have done that would've made your day much better, despite the frustration you were experiencing?

Well, I am here to tell you that you have the power to change an overwhelmingly frustrating day into a more positive and enjoyable experience, even when you thought you had no control. How can you do that? It's very simple: with your mind. Has anyone ever told you that your mind is the most powerful part of your body? This is what I want you, my dear reader, to understand. Your mindset is all you need in order to be successful in life. When you think of powerful men and women you look up to, names such as Melinda Gates, Oprah Winfrey, Michelle Obama, Barack Obama, and other influential figures may come up, and you begin to wonder: What did they do to achieve their success? Do they have bad days like me?

Here is the plain and honest truth: All of these people I've just named started by believing in themselves. The first step in believing in who you are requires you to have a positive mindset. Let me be the first to tell you that it definitely was not easy for any successful person to reach the status they have today. Everyone faces challenges in today's world, even powerful celebrities. However, having a positive mindset gives you the discipline and determination needed to persevere, even on your worst days. Your mindset is what will differentiate you as a successful person from everyone else. So, our journey will begin with the following question: How do you determine what type of mindset you have? To help you answer this, I will first help you in your quest by explaining what a mindset is.

Understanding Your Mindset

I have a very important question for each and every one of you reading this book. When you think of the word "mindset," what does it mean to you? For me, when I first began my research on mindsets and studied what it meant to me, my thoughts and feelings are what came to my mind. The more I researched, the more I discovered that my mindset is even more powerful than I realized. In fact, our mindsets have the greatest control over our reality, our emotions, and our overall mental health. If you want to be happier and healthier, then it must start from within, with the quality of your thoughts. Have you ever heard someone say, "when you believe in something, you will be able to achieve it"? What they said is most definitely true. So how do we actually define the term "mindset"?

Crum et al. (2013) explain that "a mindset is defined as a mental frame or lens that selectively organizes and encodes information, thereby orienting an individual toward a unique way of understanding and experience and guiding one toward corresponding actions and responses" (Dweck, 2008). What this definition means is that your mindset is what you use to interpret and understand information, as well as frame how you think and respond to things. To put it even more simply, your mindset is your collective sum of beliefs that shape how you see yourself and the world around you. How you feel about yourself in turn influences your behavior, your emotions, the decisions you make, and so forth.

Why Mindsets Matter

Your mindset, as we have just explained, is what determines how you perceive yourself and others, and influences how you respond to every event that occurs in your life. In addition, your mindset also includes your expectations about personal abilities and characteristics. For example, if a person believes that their shyness and anxiety in social settings is impossible to change, despite their best efforts, they will continue to be shy and anxious because they have adopted a mindset that believes those characteristics are fixed and cannot be changed.

Also, coming to recognize what your mindset is will help you to recognize how you can involuntarily contribute to your own personal disappointments.

When you understand what a mindset is, the more you are able to understand the extent to which it influences your reality. You will be amazed to discover the impact that having a positive mindset will make in your everyday living. There are two types of mindsets: a fixed mindset and a growth mindset. What is the difference? We will discuss that later on, and you will learn which type of mindset will take you from feeling frustrated to living the best possible life you ever dreamed of. I promise you, you are in for a shocking, yet revolutionary journey, as you turn the pages of this book.

Mindsets and reality

I want to share a secret with you about the world that we live in. We live in a golden era, one which we have all looked forward to and worked hard toward reaching. However, now that we are here, we often take our reality for granted. When you think of the people who have come and gone before you, can you identify what they did to be successful? I can: They all had a predetermined goal and knew where they wanted their life to go. Unfortunately, too many of us in today's society do not know where they want their lives to go, or how to take control over their reality. The definition of success has changed, and not many realize that they have the power to control how successful they are or will be in life. This is one of the main reasons why mindsets matter. Your mindset holds the key to whether you will be viewed as a failure or a success. Let me say that once more: You will become what you think about.

What Does This Mean for You?

My research has shown me that the worldview or mindset that you create for yourself greatly influences the way you live your entire life. Your mindset determines the type of person you become and dictates whether you are able to accomplish the things you desire. Many of us, including myself, have all wondered how a tiny belief has the power to transform our entire lives. Therein lies the issue, as well as what motivated me to embark on my journey of writing this book: learning more about the power of our minds. When you change your mindset, a whole new world is created for you. In this new world, a positive mindset provides a life full of success, coupled with self-validation. You have the power of choice; the power to choose what your mindset will be. Mindsets are more than just simple beliefs, as they are actually very powerful. As you read, I want you to think more about which direction you want your life to go, and which mindset will get you to that final destination.

What You Will Learn in This Book

I want to commend you for picking up this book that is focused on teaching you how to change your mindset. This simple act on your part shows that you are concerned about your mental health, and your life as a whole. When you look around you, you may notice that people who have a positive mindset live a longer and happier life when compared to those who have a negative outlook on life. Your mindset is what will either push you in the right direction or keep you back. If you do not already know which mindset to choose, this book will help you to decide. I believe we all have that hidden potential to achieve our greatest dreams; all we need to do is change our mindset and our attitudes. I have witnessed people who have been rejected for jobs or scholarships, despite having the perfect resume. What vital thing they lacked, then? A positive mindset.

This book was written for you to realize that you always had the potential to become everything you ever wanted to be, and it will show you how to do just that. I had two intentions when I wrote this book: The first was to let others know that you, the reader, are not alone, and you have a system of support. My second intention was to give you the tools that you need to take charge of your own life. You will grow as an individual, having learned about strengths, and no longer giving into negative thinking. This book is your personal weapon for changing your mindset for good. In these chapters, I will share all the information you need to know about mindsets, the different types, and the impact that they have on your life. Keep in mind that you will be challenged and inspired, but most importantly, you will learn new life-changing information.

In Chapter 1, we will discuss how complaining prevents you from living a positive life, and what you need to do to stop complaining. Chapter 2 will focus on the importance of self-validation, and why it is necessary to validate yourself as opposed to depending on others to validate you. In Chapter 3, we move on to discussing the importance of thinking responsibly; how you can use your thoughts to develop a positive attitude. Chapter 4 will highlight the importance of visualizing the life that you want and discuss strategies that you can use to begin visualizing your future. In Chapter 5, we will discuss the role of emotions and how they influence your reality. You will find out why it is important to understand how your emotions are formed, and you will also learn ways to control your emotional responses. The theme of Chapter 6 is the importance of developing a winning attitude. In it, you will learn how your mindset determines your level of success, as well as techniques that you can implement in your life to become a winner. Finally, in Chapter 7, you will learn how your actions impact reality, and the ways in which you can take back control of your reality.

How to Use This Book

I want to take this moment to encourage you to read this book in its entirety, starting from the first chapter and continuing on in the order the chapters are presented to you. Once you have completed your reading, I want you to revisit the sections that stood out to you the most and reflect on what you learned. Also, I invite you to keep a notebook with you, as there will be activities for you to help with your self-reflection and growth. The best way to complete these activities is to be completely honest with yourself at all times. I want you to get the most out of this book, and really see the change that you are looking for in your life. To really begin the process of changing your mindset, you must be committed. I am glad that I can assist you in your journey, as I genuinely believe that having a deeper understanding about mindsets is beneficial to all of us.

So, now that I have introduced what you can expect, it is time to begin our journey together. The first step is to understand one of the biggest factors that can prevent you from having a positive mindset: complaining. To start things off on the right track, I want you to reflect on the opening epigraph by Earl Nightingale, who advises us to control our thoughts. When you are able to take charge of your thoughts, you are also taking control of your life. Complaining prevents us from controlling our thoughts. You may be wondering what I mean, so without further ado, let us get started, shall we?

Chapter 1: Learn to Live and Stop Complaining

If you don't like something, change it. If you can't change it, change your attitude. Don't complain.

—Maya Angelou

By way of introduction, I am going to be completely honest about a personal trait of mine: I complain a lot. At first, I used to be embarrassed to admit that about myself. After all, would you like to be someone known for constantly complaining about things? No. What I discovered during my research in preparation for writing this book was that I wasn't alone, as we all complain daily. The even more interesting fact that I learned was that a lot of us aren't even aware when we find ourselves complaining. It is not easy to just decide one day that you want to stop complaining. Complaining actually serves a purpose, but too many of these negative conversations aren't good for you and deter you from obtaining a successful future. The best way to overcome complaining is to learn what a complaint is, the reasons why we complain, and how it impacts us mentally.

The Root of Complaints

Scott (2022) explains to us that "complaining is a natural part of human communication. It is often a response to problems or a way to communicate dissatisfaction." So, if you were expecting to never make a complaint again in your life, that would be completely unrealistic. We cannot avoid communicating, as that is how we interact and build relationships as human beings, and thus this would make complaining unavoidable. The real issue begins when we complain too much. When you complain constantly, it becomes a mental habit. In other words, over time you would find it much easier only to see the negative aspects of life. Complaining not only prevents you from enjoying and living in the moment; it influences how others think about you. To put it plainly, the more you choose to complain, the more you are telling your mind that complaining is a norm, and therefore it becomes your default reaction to everything.

Regulating Emotions

The bad thing about complaining is that the more you do it, the more stressed you feel. So here is the defining question: Why do we complain? To better understand what causes us to complain, we need to understand the factors behind it. One of the first reasons for complaining is that it helps us to regulate our emotions. Sometimes the only way that a person can manage how they feel is to vent in hopes of feeling better afterward. Let us say, for example, you are on your way to work, and you get a flat tire, and it is raining heavily, to make matters worse. You arrive at work late as a result, and you are scolded by your boss, as you missed a very important meeting. Frustrating, right? So, you call your best friend to vent about the morning from hell that you've just experienced. After complaining about everything that has happened, although you are still upset over the events of the morning, you find yourself feeling a little better, and you are able to carry on with your day. In this example, you can see how complaining is an automatic response to a frustrating experience, and it helps you get your emotions under control.

You're simply in bad mood

Another reason why many of us resort to complaining is because we are in a negative or bad mood. Using the example of the flat tire from before, a situation that makes you feel uncomfortable or ruins your plans would naturally change your positive mood into a negative one. The problem is that people tend to complain even more than they usually would whenever they are in a negative mood. In many instances, the more you find yourself complaining, the more your bad mood is increased. This creates a vicious cycle, as you remain trapped in that negative aura and unable to focus on the other positives happening around you.

It's your personality

Although it may be difficult for some of us to hear and accept, being a person who loves to complain often could naturally be a part of your personality. Psychologists believe that we have five personality traits that are collectively known as "the big five personality traits." The five broad personality traits described by the theory are extraversion/extroversion, agreeableness, openness, conscientiousness, and neuroticism (Cherry, 2021). Persons who fall under the category of neuroticism are more likely to be frequent complainers, as their personality trait is characterized by constant moodiness, irritability, sadness, and anxiety. These individuals are labeled as worriers, and struggle to regulate their emotions after stressful or difficult events. Whereas those who fall under the category of agreeableness are believed to be the least likely to complain. This is because the characteristics associated with this group are positivity and kindness, as well as people who aren't affected by negative situations.

Social groups

There is a popular Greek saying that states "show me your friends and I will tell you who you are"

(Morrison-Brandauer, 2014). In simple terms, the company that you keep influences who you are. When you are around someone who complains constantly, in turn it can motivate you to also do the same. In fact, complaining with others is actually a type of social bonding. Everyone needs the opportunity to express their frustrations, and many find it easier to do so with a close friend or family member.

G.R.I.P.E

There are five other reasons that are suggested as to why people choose to complain. These reasons are summarized using the acronym "G.R.I.P.E." These five letters stand for "Get attention, Remove responsibility, Inspire envy, Power, and Excuse poor performance" (Jane, 2016). The first reason is getting attention, and that is because people have an inner desire to be noticed by others and complaining helps them to feel acknowledged. The second reason is that when people complain about a difficult situation, it strips them of taking any responsibility to improve the situation. The third reason for complaining is that it can actually be used as a form of bragging or inspiring others to feel envious about a particular situation. The fourth reason is that when a person complains, it gives them the power to make others feel enraged also. Lastly, the fifth reason behind why people complain is that it helps them to create an excuse for their own circumstances by placing the blame on someone else.

Complaints and Mental Self-Development

As you can see from the information above, there are a variety of reasons why we complain; most importantly, it is a completely natural human reaction. The real problem occurs when we choose to complain constantly about our circumstances. The more you complain, the more it affects your mental health. It is easy to get caught up in the spell of complaining, especially in today's world. Social media, in particular, offers us an open forum in which to constantly voice our complaints. Social media platforms such as Facebook or Twitter allows users to express the thoughts in their mind, with the majority of those thoughts being consumer complaints, or simply someone venting to their followers about their day. Although this can help to relieve stress in some instances, what many fail to consider is the impact it has on our mental health.

One of the major issues with complaining that goes unnoticed is that people become too preoccupied with venting about how they feel, as opposed to finding solutions for their problems. The more we vent to express our feelings, the less attention we give to finding solutions to why we are upset in the first place. As a result, this actually makes our complaints ineffective because we are choosing to remain in the situation and merely complain about it, rather than actively look for ways to change our circumstances. When you remain stuck in whatever position it was that caused you to resort to complaining, it only results in further feelings of frustration accumulating over time. The more stressed you feel, the more likely you are to be affected by anxiety, or you may even find yourself feeling depressed.

Negative mindset

From this moment forward, I want you to always remember what I am about to tell you: Perspective is everything in life. The quality of our lives is determined by the way we look and feel about the circumstances surrounding us. When you develop the habit of being a chronic complainer, you train your brain to develop a negative mindset. If you allow complaining to remain as your primary coping mechanism, you ultimately remain stuck with a negative attitude, as your only form of relief is derived from complaining.

How to Stop Complaining and Be Happy!

I want you to take a moment and turn your attention to the quote by Maya Angelou that was used to open this chapter. I admire her words, as they beautifully capture the best way we can all stop complaining, by adjusting our attitude or mindset. It is quite simple: If there is something you do not like, then do something about it. If you are unable to change it, adjust your lens on the issue. Complaining won't fix things but changing your attitude will. So how do you adjust your attitude? The following strategies should be able to help you make the necessary changes to stop complaining.

Constructive Complaints

Trust me when I say that excessive complaining is not healthy for you, neither physically or mentally. Complaints do not make your day any better, and they do not solve whatever situation you are facing. Most importantly, you can end up stressed, and prevented from enjoying life and feeling happy. Of course, you have come to understand that it is impossible to forgo complaining in its entirety. However, what you can do is learn to complain more constructively. When you face a difficult situation, take a moment and ask yourself: "Is this worth getting upset over?" This is how you can begin to shift your mindset from a negative one to a more positive approach. Constructive criticism will help you to identify the issues that really matter and need to be addressed and learn to let go of the things that do not matter. For example, if you got to work late because of the weather and traffic, is it really worth investing your energy to complain? After all, there is nothing you can do to change the situation.

Understanding why you complain

One of the reasons we identified earlier for why we complain is that it is used as a tool to help us cope and regulate our emotions. The best way to replace our unhealthy habit of complaining excessively is to be able to identify why we do it, and the times we are most likely to complain. To get to the core of your behavior, you should practice interviewing yourself after you've complained about an issue or situation. These questions will also help to improve your ability to complain constructively, as you will be able to distinguish between a necessary and unnecessary complaint. Some questions you can ask are:

- Why do I feel this way right now?
- Was my complaint a valid one?
- Is there anything I can do to rectify the issue that I'm facing?

- Do I know anyone who can help me to solve my problem?
- Is this a one-time situation, or something that has kept on recurring?

Choosing the appropriate channel to complain

Once you are able to step back and identify the situations that are genuinely affecting you, the best way to constructively complain is to choose an appropriate channel to voice your concerns. Social media has become so powerful and integrated in our daily lives, that so many of us forget that there are boundaries we should maintain when using these platforms. Just because Facebook asks you "What's on your mind?", doesn't mean you need to answer. When we are frustrated and complaining, it is easy to say things we do not mean. The last thing you want to do is share your personal issues with your social group, and have that issue affect how they perceive you. Constructive complaining includes knowing the importance of sharing your complaints privately rather than publicly.

Stop complaining by practicing mindfulness

When you complain excessively, it prevents you from being present in the moment, and noticing the other positives that surround you. Let us all be completely honest; how much time have you spent focusing on the people around you, or the good things that happen, even when everything seems to be going all wrong? Being mindful means being aware. You can only change your mindset from complaining when you have learned to be mindful of everything that is around you. Yes, bad days do happen, but there are so many other positive things that occur that we miss, simply because we are not completely mindful or aware of our entire present.

Mindfulness involves living in the present, and not focusing on things that have already occurred, or might happen in the future. Using the example from before, if you arrive at work late because of traffic and weather, being mindful will help you to realize that this unfortunate event already happened, and the positive part is that you did eventually arrive safely to your destination. When we focus on being present, we develop a greater appreciation for being alive and able to enjoy life. The next step to practicing mindfulness is to become aware of your emotions, and how they can affect others. As said before, complaining is very contagious. You do not want to be the person who is responsible for others being in a negative mood.

Mindfulness also means learning to be appreciative and grateful for your life, including the good and bad things. Sometimes we can all take life for granted, and become self-absorbed, focusing only on the negatives. A spirit of gratitude will help you to feel happier and enthusiastic, despite any bad circumstances you face. The last step needed to practice being mindful is learning to self-reflect and take action. Take time to assess what triggers you and set some goals for how you want to improve on the way you react to difficult situations. With these goals, take time to practice how you would react the next time something occurs that triggers you. Sometimes unexpected events occur, but knowing what your weaknesses are, and being prepared to respond to the unexpected, will help you to regain your mood much quicker. Ask yourself how you can be more compassionate during a difficult situation and write down what you will do the next time something bad occurs.

Mindfulness exercises for you

It is essential for you to achieve a positive balance between your body and your mind. I want to offer five mindful exercises that you can incorporate into your daily routine, all of which don't require much effort.

1. **Observation:** This is a very powerful yet simple exercise that helps you to pay closer attention to and appreciate the environment that surrounds you. It is so easy to miss the positive things that surround us, as we focus only on the negative situations that take place. I want you to choose any object that you see daily and focus only on it for at least three minutes. Do not do anything besides looking at the object. Pretend that it is the first time you have seen this object and allow yourself to be present. Afterward, write down how taking the time to observe and be present with that object made you feel.

2. **Breathing:** This is an exercise that you can do anywhere and at any time. I want you to start breathing slowly, in and out. Make sure to breathe in and out through your nose. During this process, I want you to let go of all your thoughts. Take note of how aware you become as you breathe and eliminate everything that is on your mind.

3. **Listening:** The purpose of this exercise is to help you listen without judging, using preconceived ideas, or past experiences to influence your understanding of what is being said to you. I want you to select a song that you have never listened to before. It would be best to use headphones rather than playing

the song out loud and close your eyes as you listen to the lyrics. Listen intently, as well, to the instruments and vocals. The idea is to get you to hear the entire message first, before thinking of your response.

4. **Awareness:** The goal of this exercise is for you to become aware of the importance of your everyday tasks that you take for granted, and how simple results can make you feel more positive. I want you to think of an activity that you do every day, like washing the dishes, for example. At that moment, I want you to stop and pay attention to how you feel. Think of how blessed you are to be in the comfort of your home, and perhaps even surrounded by family.

5. **Appreciation:** This last exercise is very simple to complete. All you are required to do is identify at least six things you encounter daily that you usually would pay no notice toward. They can either be objects or people; the choice is entirely up to you. The purpose of this exercise is to help you build an appreciation for the things that may seem insignificant at first but can actually support your very existence. For instance, you had a difficult day at work, and you stop to admire the trees on your drive home. Afterward, you may be surprised to realize how calm and

positive paying attention to the little things made you feel.

Key Points to Remember From Chapter 1!

The goal of this first chapter was to introduce you to one of the most common ways that we keep ourselves back from having a positive mindset: complaining. If you want to begin the process of changing your mindset, it is best to start with one of the habits that most of us overlook every day. The key points that I want you to remember from this chapter are:

- Complaining is natural and has a role to play in our everyday communication process. It is usually how we communicate our dissatisfaction or response to a problem.
- Although complaining is unavoidable, excessive complaints can become a habit, which can lead to you developing a negative mindset.
- Some of the reasons why we complain include needing to regulate our emotions or cope with a difficult situation, being in a bad mood, or interacting socially with others who frequently complain.

- Being a chronic complainer can impact your mental health, as you will be more likely to feel stressed often or suffer from anxiety.
- Complaining does not solve our problems, but instead leaves us stuck in the situation.
- The best ways to overcome complaining are to identify why you are complaining, practice complaining constructively, and to be more mindful of your present.

Chapter 2: The Power of Self-Validation

Belief in yourself is more important than endless worries of what others think of you. Value yourself and others will value you. Validation is best that comes from within.

—Ngũgĩ wa Thiong'o

I believe we all have a unique story to share when it comes to issues with self-esteem or self-worth. Many of us can relate to how having low self-esteem has affected our lives, and what we needed to do to raise our level of self-esteem. Some of you may still be on that journey of self-improvement and self-love. Protecting your self-worth and self-esteem is your responsibility. However, sometimes when we are faced with difficult situations, it is only human for us to feel alone, and seek support and encouragement from others. Research shows that "validation is a primary human craving. We all want to be understood. We want to feel that we matter and that our thoughts and emotions matter to other people, especially to those people we care about" (LCMHCS, 2021).

Much like complaining, as we covered in the previous chapter, validation comes naturally to us.

However, it can be dangerous when we seek too much validation from other people. Depending on others to validate you as a person will lead to you relying solely on them to feel confident in who you are as a person. This also leads to a negative mindset and low self-esteem, because without external validation, you may find yourself feeling uncertain, anxious, and not worthy. So how can we avoid giving others the complete power to validate our entire existence? Ngũgĩ wa Thiong'o explains it best; you validate yourself. The best validation comes from inside. When you believe in who you are, others will believe in you also. This is the power of self-validation, and the next stage in changing your mindset from a negative to positive. In this chapter, we will now shift our attention to what is validation, why it is important, how it affects our self-esteem, and how to validate yourself. Are you ready to continue your journey? Alright, let's go!

Addicted to Validation

One of the best definitions of validation that I have found so far states that "validation is the recognition and acceptance of another person's internal experience as being valid" (Hall, 2012). When you validate someone, you are communicating that you have acknowledged how they feel. This validation is about showing another person that you have recognized their emotions, and that you are empathetic to their situation. Validation does not mean that you agree with the person, however. It is merely a means to show support and make someone else feel significant or important.

Validation and Relationships

Validation is generally most important during our developmental years of life. During childhood was when we were most impressionable, and the support from our parents helped us to recognize our inner strength. Can you remember when your parents would've praised you for accomplishing milestones, such as learning to walk or tying your shoes? That was validation. Validation is also important in adulthood, when trying to build and maintain personal relationships. Regardless of our backgrounds or gender, we long to feel understood (yes, both men and women need to feel validated). I remember a close friend of mine, we will call her Sarah, who once told me about a guy she had dated for a couple of months who was a great listener, but he was horrible at validating her feelings. Any time she related a difficult situation to him, he would sit there with a blank, emotionless face, that pretty much communicated, "are you finished?"

The breaking point of their relationship arrived one evening, when she eagerly shared the news of her promotion at work, and at the end of her story, all he had to say was "cool." That was it, a one-word response that lacked emotion or support in response to her news that she was so excited to share. What Sarah wanted, and what so many of us desire in our relationships, is that feeling of being validated; that someone else sees and understands how we feel. In all our relationships, validation is important, as it helps to satisfy that need for support and connection.

Why do we seek validation from others?

I want you to keep in mind that it is completely natural to seek validation from others. It helps us as human beings to feel accomplished, supported, and safe. When you feel accepted by someone else, it helps you to feel calm. Validation can also give you the feedback that you need, in order to feel as if you are on the right path or track. Life can be difficult for us all, and we may feel confused about choices we make. Having someone validate you may give you that boost of reassurance. Furthermore, validation can contribute to how you build your identity. It helps you to see how others view your personal traits, as well as what stands out about you. Additionally, being validated can help you form a spirit of perseverance. Whenever you are going through a stressful period, having someone acknowledge how difficult things are, and highlight how you have held your ground, can help to motivate you to continue pushing. Yes, validation can be healthy for us all when used in the right contexts.

Validation from others can also help you to create a solid foundation of self-esteem. The problem occurs when we seek too much validation externally or believe that we must be validated by others in order to feel better about ourselves. When you have feelings of low self-esteem, you tend to feel a greater need to get approval from others in order to feel better about who you are. The problem is, while there is nothing wrong with seeking approval to some extent, true acceptance can only come after you have recognized and accepted your own abilities. This is where the importance of having a positive mindset and a great self-image becomes exceedingly important. When you love yourself for you who are, you will not need to depend on the validation of others.

The Role of Self-Esteem

When you hear names such as Angelina Jolie, Serena Williams, Sam Smith, and Beyonce, what are some of the first things that come to mind? Well, for me, the words were "influential," "beautiful," and "talented." These are some of the most popular celebrities that grace magazine covers world-wide. What I didn't know, prior to all my research, was that these celebrities whom we admire have all struggled with self-esteem issues. Yes, just like me and you, the average Joes, these idolized celebs all have their moments of doubt, and times when they question their self-worth. Of course, they are faced with even more scrutiny, as their entire livelihood is in the public forum. Perhaps being constantly faced with the expectation to be perfect is why it is so easy to forget that they, too, can have issues with how they feel about themselves. They all have one mantra in common: They learned the importance of validating and loving themselves first. So, if they can do it, why not you? How do you know the signs of low self-esteem versus high self-esteem?

Signs of Low Self-Esteem

I will start by defining what self-esteem is. An eloquent definition of the term is that it "refers to the positive (high self-esteem) or negative (low self-esteem) feelings that we have about ourselves" (Stangor, 2014). What makes self-esteem such an interesting concept is the fact that it varies from person to person. In fact, "self-esteem is in part a trait that is stable over time, with some people having relatively high self-esteem and others having lower self-esteem. But self-esteem is also a state that varies day to day and even hour to hour" (Stangor, 2014). So, let us now first focus on how you can identify if you have low self-esteem. A person with low self-esteem may find themselves struggling even more to find happiness and success. This is because they perceive themselves as a victim. As they do so, it becomes easier for them to abuse themselves via self-destructive behavior such as thinking they are unlovable, accompanied by feelings of unworthiness. It is this form of mindset that results in seeking constant validation from others to feel valued.

Now that we know what self-esteem is, let's talk some more about what can cause you to have low self-esteem. Our self-image, or how we internalize what we think about ourselves, is generally the root factor. We all have a mental image of who we should be, our values, how we should behave, and even how we perceive others should feel about us. Our self-image is mostly composed of our beliefs, which have unconsciously formed over time. The issue with low self-esteem comes when you develop a negative self-image. Maybe someone once told you that you are not attractive, or perhaps you feel as if you do not deserve happiness. All these negative thoughts, including feeling dissatisfied with yourself or viewing yourself as a failure, are all signs of a low self-esteem, motivated by validation-seeking from others.

Signs of High Self-Esteem

Firstly, we should learn about everything that a high self-esteem is not. Having a positive self-image or self-esteem is not based on physical belongings, social status, or even your physical appearance. When you have a high self-esteem, it simply means that you have accepted who you are as an individual. While you may appreciate the valuation and feedback that you receive from others, you do so cautiously, as you have learned that it is more important to validate yourself, even when taking into consideration the opinions of others. The higher your self-esteem, the greater your flexibility and strength, as you are able to grow from all of your mistakes and take control of your life. High self-esteem is generally characterized by self-confidence and taking responsibility for your actions without blaming others. You are able to feel comfortable with your emotions, and aware of your weaknesses and strengths. It is important to develop a positive self-esteem as it means you love, respect, and value your own opinions, feelings, and ideas.

Negative Mindsets and Self-Esteem

By now, I'm hoping you've gained a clearer picture of how much power your thoughts have. Your worldview is influenced by your thoughts. When you think negatively, you also view your surroundings in a negative light. This is why it is important to become aware of the quality of your thoughts. Having a negative mindset could ultimately function as a self-fulfilling prophecy. If you constantly tell yourself that you are unworthy of being loved, or you're not smart enough, think about it: Wouldn't you find yourself repeating those exact words to someone else? How can you then expect someone to validate you when you doubt your own worth? Even though validation from others can prove to be valuable to some extent, the best way to overcome a negative mindset is to validate yourself.

Self-Compassion and Self-Validation

When it comes to being able to validate yourself, one of the better approaches is to treat yourself in the same way as you would treat the people closest to us, who are having some sort of difficulty or personal dilemma. What you should always bear in mind is that, regardless of whether you feel as if you've made the gravest of errors, or you're feeling a great lack of self-worth, the manner in which you treat yourself is of extreme importance. One of the first courses of action to take in becoming more compassionate would come in the form of self-realization by highlighting that not everything can be perfect, and that is okay. The sooner we are able to recognize our own struggles and lay claim to them, despite how difficult this may seem, it's a critical first step in the right direction.

When we lack compassion, especially for ourselves, this can be a deciding factor in the deterioration of our mental health conditions. It should be noted, however, that there are instances where someone can experience great difficulty in practicing self-compassion, especially after facing some sort of trauma. For example, this can occur in people who may be the aggrieved party in an affair or who may be going through a divorce, as they undergo heavy feelings of humiliation, guilt, and rejection. This heavy feeling of self-judgment is connected to diagnosing persons with anxiety, depression, and high levels of insecurity. As you can clearly see, treating yourself first with love and care is an essential pathway toward validating yourself.

Self-Validation: You Are Enough!

I want you to read the following words over and over again: You are enough. I believe that you are unique just the way you are, that you are indeed enough, and that you are the person you are meant to be. Now, I also want you to validate yourself, and remind yourself every day that you are enough. I know it can be extremely difficult, especially in our modern society, to always remember that a positive attitude and a perpetual belief in ourselves is all that we need to make ourselves happy. It is very easy to also overlook the power of valuing ourselves and become caught up in who we think the world expects us to be. So, when I say the words 'you are enough," I am encouraging you to accept yourself in this moment, with all your qualities, both good and bad. This is the power of self-validation. Self-validation is simply "the process of restoring and reinforcing the sense of self-worth, meaning of life, and personal identity and competence through a variety of activities and interactions with the natural and social environments" (Ishiyama, 1993).

Your entire life should be a process of validating yourself. It is your purpose in life to learn and recognize the value of who you are as an individual, and to learn to love your uniqueness and overall existence. When you master the art of self-validation, you generally find yourself enjoying a reality that is full of the comfort and security of self-acceptance. The process of self-validation can appear to be demanding when you have a low self-esteem, and this is why it may seem easier to seek validation from others rather than looking within. What can you do, then, to accept yourself and feel more positive about your individuality? Well, I want to highlight three useful strategies that you can implement into your daily routine to help you learn how to validate yourself. These strategies are using positive affirmations, mirror watching and positive self-talk, and starting a self-validation journal.

Positive Affirmations Make a Difference

Using positive affirmations can be an effective method of training your mind to think more positively. What makes our mind so unique is that it is unable to tell the difference between fiction and fact. When you repeat positive affirmations, you are telling your mind that what you are saying is indeed factual and true. This is one of the best strategies you can use to help boost your self-esteem, as in time, you will begin to accept that your words are the truth, and that there is no other truth. In simpler terms, affirmations are repeated positive statements that describe any desired feeling or situation and are repeated constantly in order to be registered in your mind subconsciously, to ultimately result in positive action. There are four characteristics that allow affirmations to be effective, and they are desire, conviction, attention, and interest. Take, for instance, the words I encouraged you to repeat: You are enough. That is one of the first affirmations I want you to include in your new mode of thinking.

Sometimes we create undesirable situations because we constantly repeat negative statements in our minds. When you tell yourself that you can't do something, or that you will fail, your mind accepts these negative statements as the truth, and eventually circumstances surrounding you begin to reflect your thoughts. You can transform your attitude and behavior, and work to reshape your entire life when you program your mind to believe in positive mental images. However, you should keep in mind that affirmations do not work immediately.

You must invest your attention or time, have a strong desire to see change, and make the effort each day to repeat your affirmations. You should not only wait for something negative to occur, but rather, you can engage your mind by repeating affirmations as often as you can, regardless of how your life is going at the moment. The best affirmations are stated in the present tense, as opposed to using the future tense. For example, saying "I am enough" is more effective than saying "I will be enough," as it gives the indication that you are already enough, rather than that you will be in the future. Use this strategy of creating present tense positive affirmations and write down some of your own affirmations that you can use to validate yourself.

Mirror Watching and Self Talk

If you didn't already know, I want you to know that your household mirror, wherever it is located, can help you learn to validate yourself. Each day, I want you to take a couple of minutes to look into the mirror and think of some positive words to tell yourself. You can use your positive affirmations when looking into the mirror as well. This must be done privately, and you must speak out loud. The goal is to develop the habit of loving and accepting the person who you see in the mirror. Your words feel more powerful when you repeat them while looking at yourself and learning to appreciate the person looking back at you. If you have told yourself that you are not enough, or any other thought that prevents you from appreciating who you are, a mirror conversation can help to silence those thoughts. As basic as this exercise may seem, it can help you to move away from seeking validation from others and get into the habit of praising yourself daily.

Self-Validation Journaling

Journaling is one the most therapeutic methods of changing your mindset. You can use your journal to record all the things that you are grateful for in your life and acknowledge the good or positive things that occurred for the day. Since it is so easy to spend time ruminating and complaining over what went wrong, you can use your journal to help focus on the good things you ignored while focused on the negative. List the thing that you are proud of about yourself, and acknowledge everything you've done, and then celebrate your progress. Self-validation can become a habit when you take the time to be grateful for who you are and applaud every little milestone. You can also use your journal as a prompt for your mirror watching exercise. Take a couple of minutes to list at least five things that you admire about yourself. Then stand in front of your mirror and repeat that list to yourself. In this way, journaling can help you to regain your self-confidence when you feel low. It will help you to build self-compassion, and it provides a forum to remind you every day that you are doing great.

Key Points to Remember From Chapter 2!

It is only natural for us, as humans, to seek validation from others. However, seeking too much validation is generally the sign of a negative mindset. So, here are the key points you should remember from this chapter in order to improve your mindset:

- Constant validation seeking is unhealthy, and you may find yourself becoming a slave to it, as your existence becomes dependent on what others think about you.
- You must be able to accept and understand yourself first, as this will improve your mental self-development.
- Having a high self-esteem helps you to love and appreciate who you are and will cause you to rely less on validation from others.
- Self-validation helps you to create a positive mindset, have greater self-esteem, and believe in who you are and in your abilities.

- You can practice self-validation by beginning to use positive affirmations daily, using positive self-talk in front of the mirror, and creating a journal dedicated to validating your strengths.

Chapter 3: Responsible Thinking Shapes Your Reality

Accepting complete responsibility for your life means that you refuse to make excuses or blame others for anything in your life that you're not happy about.

—Brian Tracy

I am excited that you have gotten this far in your journey of learning how to change your mindset. Why am I so excited? Because I have great news to share with you: I want you to tell you that you are in control. Yes, you have complete control over your reality. Before you can gain complete control over your reality, however, it is imperative that you understand how critical your thoughts are in shaping your reality. Our realities are determined by three factors: the quality of our thoughts, our emotions, and actions. So far, this book has intended to give you a deeper insight into how your thoughts, specifically as they relate to complaining and self-validation, can affect your reality. Now that we have discussed the importance of the quality of thoughts, we can move forward into how you can change your thinking.

It all begins with thinking about responsibility and accepting responsibility over your life and reality. What does responsible thinking mean, you may be wondering? Well, I loved the words captured by Brian Tracy in the epigraph above, as they eloquently express the core of responsible thinking and the main focus of this chapter. As Tracy suggests, when you accept complete responsibility for your life, you are refusing to blame others or make excuses for any elements that interfere with your happiness. This is why I said that you have control, as you can choose how you feel about life simply by thinking responsibly. Remember in Chapter 1, when we discussed how one of the reasons why we complain is due to the need to blame others? This is the complete opposite of responsible thinking and is behavior that someone with a positive mindset should steer clear of. So, without further delay, I want to discuss how you can now make the change to think responsibly and regain control over your reality. This chapter will begin by explaining how your thought process works, and how you can pay attention to your thoughts. We will also discuss, in deeper detail, what we mean by positive thinking, and how you can change your negative perspectives into positive ones. Are you ready to think responsibly? Alright, I believe you are, so let's have some fun!

Understanding Your Thought Process

The first step in responsible thinking is making sure that your thoughts are in alignment with what you want for yourself. If you want to be successful or happy, then you must ensure that the quality of your thoughts fall within that framework. I am positive that you want to be happy or successful for the entire duration of your life, rather than just for a temporary period. Therefore, changing the nature of your thoughts must be a goal that you commit to for the long-term. Thinking responsibly should never be a temporary practice, in which you obtain the positivity and peace of mind you desired for just a short time, then revert back to your prior thinking habits. Thinking responsible is a state of mind; it should be your permanent way of living, and a process that remains ongoing to ensure that you are successful.

When you think about your role models and their successes, have you ever stopped to wonder why they are able to continuously achieve more milestones? The answer is simple: It's because they were able to take responsibility for their own future. Even though to you they may appear to be successful, to them, they still have much more to accomplish. The process of responsible thinking is a journey that never ends.

You have to keep working and improving yourself. So now, the next step is to get a better understanding of what is meant by the term "thought process."

Defining Your Thought Process

When I say thought process, I am simply referring to the way in which your mind functions. Specifically, is your mind's functioning positive or negative? Your thought process is composed of your routine of thinking, how you view various situations, and how you interpret scenarios, circumstances, or conditions. Have you ever stopped to analyze how you view the circumstances that surround your life—especially the negative events that have occurred? Think: How did you respond to those events? How did your mind function when those events took place? How have you trained your mind to respond when events of a similar nature occur? Do your thoughts work out in your favor, or do you find that your thoughts work against you, resulting in you feeling anxious or stressed? These are some of the factors that must be considered when you analyze your thoughts. Moving right along, we will shift our focus to learning more about the different categories of thought process.

Categories of thought process

There are a wide variety of thought processes, but in this chapter, we will focus on the main ones. These include introspection, contemplation, and divergent thinking. These are the ones that you need to learn in order to exercise the most control over your reality.

Introspection: This thought process involves the role of note taking and analyzing your emotions and thoughts. The goal is to pay more attention to your thoughts in order to further understand your actions, and why you think about things in a specific way. As we covered so far, your thoughts directly influence your actions, so you need to get to the root of your thoughts. It is only at this root that you can understand why you behave in certain ways, or how you feel about certain situations. This thought process provides you with the ideal opportunity to identify your negative thoughts that affect you, and work on erasing them. You get the chance to completely change those negative thoughts and replace them with positive ones that will help you to feel better about your life.

Introspection helps you to gain more control over emotions, as you can decide to only think positively, regardless of external circumstances. Whenever you are faced with difficult situations that may deter you from accepting responsibility for the situation, ask yourself the following questions: How would feeling sad about the situation bring me any good? Why would I choose to blame someone else for my own problems? What can I do to help myself feel better? When you are able to ask yourself questions that challenge you to see how your perspective is only keeping you back, it will help you to realize that negative thinking only makes the situation worse.

Contemplation: I am sure that all of us—yes, myself included—spend hours every day contemplating different scenarios, and what their outcome may be. For the most part, it is hard for any of us to ever truly decide what we should or shouldn't do in certain situations. Take, for example, if you have a first date planned with someone you've just met, and you find yourself contemplating where to go, what to wear, what to talk about, and so on. When you have reached a place of mental confusion regarding what the best decisions are, this is usually where you begin to contemplate.

Contemplating is a thought process that can drastically influence the outcome of your present reality and future. For example, say you want to make a change in your career, and you are contemplating whether you should start your own business or apply for a different position in a new company. You may find yourself thinking negatively about the outcome, and thus you may delay yourself from making a choice. Or, if you choose to not contemplate over what is the best choice to make, you may rush, and end up making a decision without analyzing how the outcome of that decision can affect you. Remember, that responsible thinking involves accepting responsibility for your actions, but you must also be conscious of the decisions that you make. This thought process gives you the power to think responsibly in a more conscientious manner. Sometimes we may already know the decision that we would like to make, but because we have wired our brains to think negatively, we do not act on inner desires. When you contemplate, it helps you to feel more secure in knowing that you have made the best choice, and therefore you feel more confident about the outcome. Some questions that you can ask yourself when contemplating are: How will my decision benefit me? Are there any risks that I should consider? Will this decision help me to reach my goals? Questions like these will help you to move forward in a positive manner and allow you to grow.

Divergent thinking: This is a unique thought process, in which you analyze your assumptions about how life should be. We all have preconceived notions about how certain aspects of our lives must be carried out, and we live our lives in alignment with these beliefs that we have created for ourselves. For example, one might think that a normal way of life includes getting an education, getting a job, and only then focusing on building a family. Divergent thinking is where you challenge the beliefs that you have accepted as usual or normal and look at other alternatives that can help you to be more positive. For instance, there may be those that believe that in order to be successful, they must be alone, or it is impossible to find someone who makes them happy. For them, this is their usual way of life. With divergent thinking, you can gain better clarity as to why you feel this way and realize that being alone is a product of thinking negatively, and you can actually be successful when surrounded by loved ones.

Paying Attention to Your Thoughts

I came across an ancient Chinese proverb that, to this date, is still relevant and influential. The saying is as follows:

> Be careful of your thoughts, for your thoughts become your words. Be careful of your words, for your words become your actions. Be careful of your actions, for your actions become your habits. Be careful of your habits, for your habits become your character. Be

careful of your character, for your character becomes your destiny (GoodReads, n.d.).

As you should be able to tell from this quote, it reinforces what we have covered from the very beginning of this book: Your thoughts are powerful, and they influence the entire outcome of your life, the person that you will become, and, overall, how happy you will feel about where your life takes you. Our thoughts, along with how we express them, are what shape our reality and destiny. Even if we do not feel comfortable with this fact, it is the reality of life. Our thoughts shape everything. The more you pay attention to your thoughts, the more control you have over your character, and ultimately your entire destiny. It's almost overwhelming to know just how much power your mind actually has, isn't it? This is why it is so important to pay attention to the quality of your thoughts.

In order to establish whether you have a negative mindset or a positive mindset, you need to pay attention to the quality of your thoughts. How do you complete this task? You can begin by being more conscious of what and how you think. The goal is to identify when your negative thoughts begin to appear, what triggers these thoughts, and how frequently you experience these negative feelings. The more aware you are of what goes on internally, and the cause, the more it will help you to gain better control of how you look at things. The next step is to give your thoughts a name. When a situation occurs, pay attention to how you feel, and give those thoughts a name. Are they positive or negative? Doing this will help you be more aware of your thoughts in the present, as well as helping you move on to the next step more smoothly—that of replacing your thoughts. If you identify that in a certain moment you are experiencing negative thinking—for instance, say you are scared of facing a job interview—then you have now rightly named this as negative, and you can now focus on choosing a more positive thought to replace the negativity with. Remember how we discussed using affirmations to validate yourself? This can also help you to replace your negative thoughts with positive ones too.

Responsible Thinking Is Positive Thinking

I have mentioned the words "positive thinking" repeatedly so far, but do you actually know what they mean, and how to begin thinking positively, if you haven't been doing so all along? Positive thinking is all about your attitude. It is a choice not to dwell on the negative aspects of life, but rather to focus on the good, regardless of the events that surround you. When you expect good things to occur, and you feel optimistic about these good things coming to pass, then you are thinking positively. This does not mean that you disregard the various obstacles that you may face along the way, however. Positive thinking is simply choosing to believe that good things can occur, despite the many challenges that may arise along the way.

Deeply consider the following definition of positive thinking: "positive thinking is a mental and emotional attitude of expecting good and favorable results, and not getting discouraged when plans do not proceed as expected. It means trying over again and not accepting defeat" (Sasson, n.d.). Or another helpful definition states, "positive thinking is a mental attitude in which you expect good and favorable results. In other words, positive thinking is the process of creating thoughts that create and transform energy into reality" (leadingpersonality, 2013). From both perspectives provided, we should be able to see how thinking positively can shape our reality.

I want you to always keep the following words in mind long after you've finished reading this book: You can have a reality that is full of upliftment and joy if you make the decision to think positively. When you think positive thoughts, your actions reflect those thoughts, and there is nothing more responsible than taking control of your reality and making the decision to be happy and successful. You can choose to be a complainer, or you can seek validation from others, or you can even choose to be happy even on your worst days and feel better about who you are. The choice is all yours. However, I believe—and I know you do, also—that it will benefit you more to think positively. The more positive you are, the more you stand out as a person. This is what draws others to you. Thinking positively is a magnet, as "others know us by our character. It's our stamp of individuality" (Jameson, 2014). Wouldn't you like to stand out as an individual, as well? It all begins with changing your present perspective.

Changing Your Perspective

Some of us wake up every day feeling as if nothing changes. After all, it's a new day, but won't it be just like all the days that have come before it? Your routine remains the same, and you cannot see how things could ever change. I am sorry, but the last thing I want for you to do is remain stuck, thinking that you cannot change the direction of your life. I need you to understand that when you change the way you think, you are opening yourself up to a whole new world of possibilities. This is your moment to change your point of view and allow new habits to develop. You can change your perspective by taking back the power you have relinquished over your thoughts. When you complain, blame others, or wait on validation from someone, you remain stuck in a zone where you do not realize that you always had control over your own reality. For example, if you tell yourself that someone is more charismatic and charming than you will ever be, you are convincing yourself that you will never be able to be charismatic whatsoever. Changing your perspective will allow you to see that you may never have the exact qualities someone else has, but you have qualities that make you remarkable as well. This is how you take ownership of who you are and focus on the negative attitudes that you want to change.

Converting Negative Beliefs Into Positives

So, now we have reached the stage where you may be wondering what you can do to transform your thinking from negative to positive. It is important to remember that no matter how small a negative thought may be, the more you allow it to develop, the more it can take control of your entire mindset. To begin the process of developing positive thinking habits, I want you to assess how much of your time you have devoted to feeling happy every day. How much time do you spend complaining and focusing on yesterday's events? When you are a positive thinker, being happy becomes your goal, as well as your worldview. This is how you think responsibly, and ultimately shape your reality—by making the conscious choice to be optimistic about your life. Think about it this way: "There are 3,600 seconds in an hour and 57,600 seconds in a normal 16-hour waking day. If we have one thought per second, then we have about 60,000 thoughts in one day. What percentage of your 60,000 thoughts led to positive emotions and what percentage to negative ones?" (Stevens, 2010).

As you can see, the majority of our time is spent thinking each day, so the more time you invest in being positive, the easier it will become to develop and maintain a positive mindset. You can begin the process of converting your negative beliefs by keeping a mental log of your thoughts and emotions. Identify which thoughts were associated with negative emotions as they occur. Also, try to pay attention to the quality of thoughts you had that preceded any negative emotions you feel. Then, you can move forward by listing those negative emotions that reoccur. For example, do you constantly worry about your finances? Or do you have a fear of being rejected or alone? What caused these beliefs to occur? Once you have identified these beliefs, you can create a plan for how to overcome these emotions. For instance, maybe your fear of rejection was triggered by a social media post. After introspection, you can then decide how to utilize social media in a way that doesn't cause unnecessary negative feelings. The power is in your hands; you get to decide what makes you feel positive.

Choose to be happy

The more I researched about positive mindsets, all my findings led me to a final conclusion: that our happiness, our mental self-development, and even how long we are blessed to live life on this earth, are not determined by the circumstances or events that we experience daily. Instead, the way we feel and think about who we are is the main supporting factor. Many of us use social media platforms such as Facebook or Twitter, and we may find ourselves spending a great deal of time on these platforms, which leaves us feeling bad or guilty. Have you ever stopped to wonder about why using Facebook makes you feel these things? Well, it is because we tend to compare our personal lives to others, and the most attractive parts of peoples' lives are usually what gets posted on social media. So, of course, some of us may feel as if our lives could never measure up to the level of success that these people seem to demonstrate online. This is one of the many ways you can develop a negative mindset.

You must choose to be happy with your own life first, and not compare your journey to someone else's. Having a positive mindset can sometimes come more naturally to others, but the goal is to always remember that happiness is a choice. Instead of increasing your anxiety by comparing your life or your accomplishments to those of other people, try to focus more on the small changes that occur every day in your own life. Happiness is all about making a personal effort. You must persevere and fight to be happy. If having positive thoughts does not come easy for you, then you have to work to achieve your happiness. Practice finding the silver lining every day.

Key Points to Remember From Chapter 3!

To round off this chapter, I want to reemphasize that your mind is one of your most powerful weapons, and that you are in control of your own reality. Making the choice to think responsibly and be more positive is a choice that only you can make. To begin your commitment of thinking responsibly, you should keep the following key points from this chapter in mind:

- The quality of your thoughts ultimately controls and shapes your destiny. To regain control over your reality, it is your responsibility to change your mindset.

- Responsible thinking involves accepting your life for what it is, and where you are. Responsible thinking also includes being optimistic or thinking positively about your life's path.

- To develop a positive mindset, you must understand what a thought process is, and the different ways in which you can process your emotions and thoughts. Paying attention to your thought process is crucial, as your thoughts control your actions and habits, which all become a part of your character.

- Thinking positively depends on your attitude. You can change your negative attitude into a more positive attitude by being aware of what triggers your negative emotions and replacing negative statements with positive statements.

Chapter 4: Visualize the Life You Want

Winners in life visualize their success and look forward to reaping and enjoying the rewards of their accomplishments. They revel in their hard-earned victory, and that reinforces their superior level of self-confidence.

—Lorii Myers

Now that we have gained a better understanding of the power of our thoughts, combined with how to think responsibly by developing a positive mindset, it is time to make an action plan for the life you want to live. If you always wanted to be successful and happy, you actually now have the opportunity to make that happen, and it all starts with visualizing the life you want. This is the next stage in changing your mindset: Learning about the power of visualization. Visualization is not a new concept, in fact, many of the business entrepreneurs and celebrities that we look up to as successful role models accredit visualization as a factor behind their successes. Have you heard of the name Jim Carrey? I'm sure you have, as he is most popular these days for movies such as *The Incredible Burt Wonderstone* and *Sonic the Hedgehog*. However, he wasn't always as popular as he is now. In fact, if you were to ask anyone in the year 1990 who Jim Carrey is, they wouldn't have even heard of the actor. In one of his many interviews, he explained how he used visualization to help him reach where he wanted to be. He went on to say that he visualized himself receiving checks amounting to ten million dollars every day for a period of four years. Not too long after, he would go on to receive a check for ten million dollars for his role in the 1994 blockbuster movie *Dumb and Dumber* (Hoffman, 2019). Incredible, isn't it?

This is what I want for you to accomplish after reading this chapter: I want you to be able to use the power of visualization to create the life that you've always wanted—the one you've kept yourself back from. This chapter's epigraph by Lorii Myers effectively summarizes what visualization is all about; winners who visualize their success spend their lives looking forward to when they can enjoy their accomplishments. You have to train your mind to see the future that you want for yourself. In this chapter, we will explore exactly what visualization is, and how you can avoid self-sabotaging your vision. We will also discuss methods on how you can learn to visualize the future you've always dreamed of. Now that you know what is in store for you, let us begin with learning more about visualization.

The Power of Visualization

It is truly fascinating to observe how much power the mind has, and how it leads to incredible changes when you adapt to having a positive mindset. I love to see others put visualization to the test, and become amazed when they witness first-hand the difference this makes. As you learned in the previous chapter, our minds can't tell the difference between reality and what is imagined. The words that you choose to believe in are what will become your reality, which is why I emphasized the importance of thinking responsibility and having an optimistic or positive outlook. This process of telling our minds what to think is known in the scientific realm as neuroimaging. According to psychologists, neuroimaging works by the person thinking or visualizing a specific event in their minds. The more they repeatedly visualize the event, eventually, it will occur or become their reality. This is the foundation upon which visualization is based, creating your reality with your mind.

Exactly What Is Visualization?

So, how do we define this unique concept of visualization? Firstly, visualization, or creative visualization as it is called by others, is a mental technique in which you use your imagination to create your goals. The idea is that you are able to attract your goals into your life when you visualize them occurring. For some, visualizing is simply daydreaming, but it is more powerful than that. Visualization helps you to boost the confidence and drive you need to pursue your goals, because you have already visualized how it will feel when you accomplish what you've set out for. Even when you may find it hard to create the change you need in your life, visualization dares us to think bigger. The only limitations that we actually experience are the ones that we have in our minds. When you visualize the life you want, you are giving yourself the power that you need to be stronger than your self-imposed limitations. The only thing that you must change in your life is your outlook—nothing else. The more you are able to examine things in another light, the more it will help you to propel your future toward the direction that you want.

The Role of Self-Sabotage

Of course, the only factor that can limit our ability to visualize a successful future is when we self-sabotage our visions. It is very easy to feel afraid of failing, and we can destroy our visions before giving them a chance by having a negative mindset. When we self-sabotage our visions, we are actively taking steps that prevent us from reaching the very same goals that we set for our lives. It all comes back to having a low self-esteem, not believing in ourselves, and engaging in negative self-talk.

Face the Truth That We All Self-Sabotage

I do not want you to be too hard on yourself, because the reality is that we are all prone to self-sabotaging thinking and actions. At some point in our lives, we have either passively or actively behaved in a self-sabotaging way or told ourselves we are incapable of doing something that we wanted to. Much like complaining, self-sabotage is a natural part of being human. The great news is, when you are able to identify that you are indeed engaging in self-destructive behavior, you can learn how to cut out the actions that you are doing that are keeping you back. The only way to determine this is for you to know exactly what self-sabotage is, why you self-sabotage, and how to identify when you are self-sabotaging your future.

What is self-sabotage?

Self-sabotage is any unconscious or conscious behavior that we carry out that destroys us emotionally, mentally, or physically, and prevents us from achieving success in our personal lives. Self-sabotage undermines your values and goals and affects your overall well-being as it stems from having a negative mindset. The main characteristics of self-sabotage are negative self-talk, as well as being disorganized and indecisive. Trying to be completely perfect in everything you do is another form of self-sabotage, as you are pushing yourself to achieve an unrealistic goal. Self-sabotage results in lowering your self-confidence and actively preventing you from achieving any goal you may visualize. It can also result in you feeling stuck or trapped in your present reality.

Why do we self-sabotage?

Self-sabotage can occur for a variety of reasons. For most people, self-sabotage is linked to a negative outlook. People who have low confidence or are affected by self-hatred tend to engage more in self-sabotaging behavior. Self-sabotage can also be a coping mechanism. When a person doubts their ability to achieve their needs, they may resort to sabotaging their own lives. For instance, there are people who desire to be in a relationship, but are deeply afraid of being alone, and may sabotage their relationships instead because they believe they are incapable of finding the relationship that they truly desire. Another reason people resort to self-sabotage is to avoid taking responsibility for their lives, and healing from the pain of their past. Visualizing the life that you want requires being happy, healthy, and excited about your future. When you practice self-sabotage, you are also engaging in negative self-talk where you tell yourself that you don't have what it takes to put yourself back out there. Your life is completely dependent on what you think about yourself, as well as how you feel about your life overall. Self-sabotaging behaviors prevent you from seeing the positives in your life and hinders you from imagining the many more good things that you can achieve.

Another reason why a person might self-sabotage is because they lack self-worth. If you do not believe in yourself and your capabilities, then you can't achieve the goals you have visualized. Lack of confidence and self-worth tells a person that they cannot reach their full potential. When you combine a lack of self-worth with a fear of success, you are more likely to engage in self-sabotaging behavior that will hinder your success. The closer you get to achieving your vision will result in you self-sabotaging in order to avoid achieving that goal.

Roadblocks to Visualization

Now that you know what visualization is, and how we can self-sabotage our own lives, we also need to explore deeper the factors that prevent us from visualizing the best lives possible for ourselves. Two of the main reasons why people may find it impossible to create a vision is because they make excuses, and they let their past define their reality.

Stop making excuses!

When you make excuses, it becomes literally impossible to be good at anything else. I want to take another moment and reflect honestly on your past actions. How often have you found yourself creating excuses when things in your life didn't turn out the way you wanted? Did you resort to complaining or refusing to take responsibility for your circumstances? Have you ever used past failures as your reason why you couldn't or wouldn't be able to do something in the future? If you have, these are all classic signs that your life is based on excuses. This is counterproductive to visualizing the life that you want. When you make excuses, it prevents you from being able to live to your fullest potential.

Visualization requires you to be positive and imagine all the things that you are about to accomplish in your life.

If visualizing is a form of dreaming about what you want to achieve, then excuses are almost dreamed up statements that we create to prevent us from taking action. We have reasons for why we make excuses, with the main reason usually being that we have a negative mindset. Once again, you are witnessing the importance of the quality of your thoughts and thinking positively. To get rid of excuses, you have to be able to acknowledge your fears. To overcome the need of resorting to excuses, you must be able to admit that this is a trait you have. Begin by asking yourself: What are some of the excuses I make, and why? Reflect on how these excuses make you settle for things as opposed to obtaining what you truly want.

Do not let your past define you!
The next factor that can prevent anyone from visualizing the life they truly want is when they refuse to accept their past. The rules are very simple: You simply do not have the power to change anything that has already occurred; however, you do have the power to change your future. When you visualize, you are giving yourself that power to shape your future. The goal is to realize and accept the role that

your past has played in shaping the person you are today. It has brought you to where you are now, but now you have the golden ticket to change your destination, by establishing a vision for where you would like your life to head. When you allow your past to control your present, it makes it harder to commit to future goals. I want you to realize that your past only serves one purpose, and that is to be a memory. Your memories must not be allowed to influence your future. You deprive yourself of harnessing the full power of visualization when you give past outcomes more attention than you should.

How to Visualize Your Reality

So, you've made the decision to embark on visualizing the life you want, and now you may be wondering; how do I accomplish that? Visualizing is easy, and most importantly, it can be a lot of fun. You begin by establishing a specific vision or goal. When you imagine your future, picture yourself as having already accomplished your goal. I want you to imagine the scenario with as much detail as you can muster. Engage your senses into your visual, and think about emotions you are feeling, and the people you are surrounded by. Now tell me, doesn't it feel magical? I will discuss a bit more on how to establish your vision, as well as how to support your visualization with affirmations, and also how to create a vision board.

Establish your vision

If you want to truly be successful, you must know exactly where you want to go. That is the purpose of visualization, and what will guide you every day. Your vision is what gives you a sense of direction, and a destination that you must reach. I once listened to a podcast that featured the renowned United States Olympian swimmer Michael Phelps, as he discussed how visualization helped him to be successful and reach his goal of winning gold in the Olympics. He explained that it is incredibly important to visualize the path you want for your future, as well as how you plan on accomplishing that goal, and the person that you would like to become. When you fantasize or dream about the life you want for yourself, you are actually ridding yourself of any doubts, and envisioning your soon to be reality. Michael Phelps encouraged listeners to write down their visions, and to create exciting visions that encourage them to want to get out of their beds every morning. Your vision is something that must be lived daily and incorporated into everything that you do. He concluded his interview by reinforcing that your vision must be your daily mission.

After listening to this interview, I felt as if he had described thoroughly what the core of visualization is all about: You can be successful when you create a routine. Your vision is how you create that routine or roadmap toward success. Establishing your vision involves setting a standard for yourself, and how you would like to live. I have asked various people over the years what their purpose or vision was, and let me say, I was genuinely surprised by how many were unable to tell me what their vision was. In fact, many of my colleagues and friends admitted that they never stopped to think of how they would like their life to be, as they have been trained to think that certain life changes are simply impossible. I want to pause for a moment here, to tell you that this is your chance, right now, to establish your vision for your life. If you've never taken the time to sit and really reflect on how you speak to yourself, and the words that you use that shape your future, now is the perfect opportunity.

The best way I can describe how to begin establishing your vision is to compare your life to a car. Do you think that a car can reach its destination if the driver does not know where they are going? Definitely not! Your vision is your own personal map that provides the clarity you need in order to establish where your life is headed, and what you need before you can even get started. When you are unable to establish your own vision for your life, you give others the power to control where you are headed. The issues of seeking validation from others that we discussed previously becomes more significant, as you resort to the opinion of others to provide the direction that you need. Your vision is what gives you complete control over your own reality.

Questions to help you establish your vision

Establishing your vision all comes back down to the quality of your thoughts. You can't create a successful vision if you have a pessimistic outlook on your life. You must be able to identify your values and recognize what you are passionate about in your life. Take the time to stop complaining, and reflect on who you are and what makes you happy, and then ask yourself the following questions to help you create your vision:

1. What matters the most to you in your life?
1. Can you think of anything that would bring you more happiness in your life?
2. Do you know what you really care about in life?
3. Do you know what your talents are?
4. Can you identify the traits that make you special?

5. What aspects would you like to see being more present in your life?
6. What legacy would you like others to remember you by?

Visualize with affirmations

In Chapter 2, we discussed how you can use positive affirmations to help you self-validate and think more positively. Positive affirmations are also very effective when used to support what you visualize for your life. For instance, if you were to affirm that you are the manager of your own company, in this statement you are visualizing that you become the successful leader of your own business. By using affirmations as a form of support, they can help you to remain focused on your vision and remain motivated to achieve what you have visualized for your life.

Creating your vision board

Now that you have established your vision, the next step is to remain committed to making your visualization a reality. A useful way in which you can achieve this is to create a vision board, or what others refer to as a "vision map." This vision board will be your visual and physical representation of the vision that you have established for your life. How often you create a vision board is entirely up to you, as some people create one at the start of each year and make amendments during the course of the year. This is your chance to be as creative as you would like to be and design your board to your liking. You can use affirmations, stories or pictures, or anything else that would help you to remain focused on your vision.

Visualization exercise

I want to help you learn how to look toward your future. I discovered an activity during my research that I practiced, and it helped me to remain focused. When you are unable to see the road that is ahead of you, it is natural to feel afraid. However, it is the fear of the unknown that can ultimately hinder all your progress. You must be able to create a visual so powerful that your mind has something beautiful to focus on. So, let us practice creating that powerful image right now. I want you to find a room that is comfortable, and that is preferably without any interruptions. You need to give yourself space and privacy to ensure that you feel relaxed. In this private moment, you are giving your mind the freedom to daydream, letting your innermost thoughts come to the forefront of your mind. Let your mind speak to you and tell you your deepest desires, and let it describe the way you can achieve these things. I want you to use this space to give yourself complete permission to believe in the power of your dreams.

If you find yourself feeling stuck, or you are unable to create a clear and powerful vision, try using the following questions to guide you:

1. What would my ideal life look like?
2. What do I feel passionate about?
3. What things make me feel as if I have a purpose in my life?
4. How does my career make a difference in my life?
5. If I did not have to worry about money, what would be some of my goals?
6. What are some things I would wish for to come true?
7. Why do I want this goal so badly?
8. What do I want others to remember about me?

Key Points to Remember From Chapter 4!
It might be hard to accept, but sometimes the only thing holding us back in our lives is nothing more than, well, ourselves. For many of us, there can be a wide gap between where we are and where we would like to be in life. The information provided to you in this chapter has shown you that by visualizing the life you want; you are helping yourself to reduce that gap. To end things off as we continue on with our

discussion, I want to remind you of the key points that we covered in this chapter:

- Visualization is a mental technique that you can use to create the life you want for yourself. When you visualize or imagine a goal, you picture yourself as having already achieved that goal. Training your mind to believe something by visualizing it is how you determine your reality.
- For visualization to be effective, you must think responsibly and engage in positive self-talk.
- Self-sabotaging behaviors, making excuses for yourself, or refusing to accept your past are all roadblock that prevent you from visualizing the life that you want.
- In order to make visualization a success, you must first establish what your vision is. To support your vision for the life you want, you should create a vision board or map, and use positive affirmations.

Chapter 5: Control Your Emotions and Your Reality

We cannot control what emotions or circumstances we will experience next, but we can choose how we will respond to them.

—Gary Zukav

In the previous chapters, we've more or less been able to establish the universal truth that you are what you think you are. As much as you've come to realize how powerful your thoughts are, there is another element combined with our thoughts that is equally as powerful and influential: That element is your emotions. Whenever you think of something, it triggers an emotional reaction or response. That emotional response, in turn, influences how you act and perceive the circumstances surrounding you. For instance, if you regularly think to yourself that you are not worthy, then you may feel emotions of unworthiness or depression. Your body will also react to your emotions, as is usually displayed via your facial expressions or posture. However, if you were to think more empowering and positive thoughts, for example, saying that you are a success, then you would find that your emotional state becomes more positive. Our mental thoughts reaffirm our emotions, and together they form a specific cycle in which you think, feel, and think, and then it repeats.

If you can recall, I would've explained that your reality is determined by the quality of your thoughts, your actions, and your emotions. We've already discussed in detail the relationship between your thoughts and your reality, and now it's time to shift your attention to how your emotions influence your reality. Gary Zukav shows us via his words in the epigraph to this chapter, that even if you are unable to control the emotions you will experience next, you can, at least, control how you respond to them. In this chapter, we will take a closer look at what emotions are and why they are important to us. We will also discuss how you can learn to control your emotional responses and regain control over your life. I want to give you some important advice before you proceed to read this chapter, and that advice is as follows: Your emotions are temporary; they do not last forever. So, always remember that how you respond to your emotions in the moment could have a long-lasting effect. You'll understand why I said this shortly. Let's continue.

Emotional Control Is Yours for the Taking

Without the shadow of a doubt, your mind is the most unique part of your body. It has its own place, and it can make your life a haven if you are able to control your thoughts and emotions. Every day of our lives, we all experience a variety of emotions. Even during my process of writing this book, I experienced both low and high emotions. For the most part, I was so overjoyed and excited that I had the opportunity to provide others with a useful tool that would help them to understand the way they think and feel, as well as the impact it could have on their lives. I felt content knowing that my readers' lives would drastically improve after reading this book. I felt motivated and couldn't help but visualize how successful the book would turn out to be. However, after my initial period of excitement, when it came down to putting pen to paper and writing the actual book, I noticed that all the excitement I felt disappeared. The ideas that I had visualized as being so great had lost their appeal. I felt as if writing was boring, and the material I had to contribute was not valuable.

With each passing day, I found writing to be more of a challenge, and my confidence dropped. After all, how was I to write a book about mindsets and emotions if I was ruminating in my own pool of self-doubt? Ironic, isn't it? What I eventually realized was that this book was my special opportunity to work on improving my own mindset, and practice how I could respond to my negative emotions. This is why I chose to share this story with you, because we all experience negative emotions. On any given day, we can feel both high and low. I certainly did. As I said in the opening paragraph of this chapter, emotions are temporary. When you remember that what you feel is unique to that moment in time, it will help you learn what to do with the moments that you feel low. Instead of beating yourself up over negative emotions, you can use your emotional state to help you grow as a person. This is how you can control your reality—by using your emotions to improve yourself.

I want to take this moment, as we begin our discussion about emotions, to ask you the following question: Can you tell how you are feeling at this very moment? In order to take control of your emotions, you must be able to identify how you feel. I've noticed that many people are no longer in touch with their feelings. It is easy to become disconnected with your feelings because too many of us do not talk about our emotions. I asked you to assess how you feel right now because it is critical that you understand that your feelings are what will determine the quality of your life. Your emotions can make you feel miserable or uninspired, or they can make your life feel magical. Your emotions guide you and alert you to when things are wrong in your life and allow you to make the necessary changes to feel better. The reason why it is hard for most to control their emotions, is simply because they never learned how to talk about what they are feeling. This is about to change. To help you get in touch with your emotions, you need to learn, first, what emotions even are.

Getting in Touch With Your Emotions

Have you ever taken the time to wonder what emotions are, and what role they serve in your life? Emotions are a shared universal human experience. The six basic types of emotions that we have all experienced are happiness, fear, anger, sadness, surprise, and disgust. Cherry (2013) explains that "an emotion is a complex psychological state that involves three distinct components: a subjective experience, a physiological response, and a behavioral or expressive response."

Subjective experience: Even though we all experience the basic types of emotions, this is still regarded as a subjective experience due to our various cultural and social backgrounds. Also, we all react differently and in various extremes to different situations. For instance, all anger isn't the same, as one person may feel slightly annoyed, whereas another may become blinded by rage and respond violently to a situation.

Physiological response: Have you ever noticed that when you feel afraid or anxious, your heart rate increases, or there is a tight feeling in your stomach? Our bodies also experience a physiological response to the emotion that we are feeling.

Behavioral or expressive response: This component refers to how you express your emotion. For example, you may find yourself smiling whenever you feel happy, or you may frown or cry when you are feeling sad.

Ego and emotions

Another factor that shapes your emotions is your ego. To be able to learn how to control your emotions, you also need to learn what an ego is, and how it functions. Okay, trivia question: Have you ever heard the song by Beyonce called "Ego," where she sings "I got a big ego"? What do you think the term ego refers to? When we use the word ego, we are referring to our self-identity that we have created for ourselves via our thoughts. It is how you identify your beliefs and traits. Some people may not be aware of their ego, as your understanding is influenced by how self-aware you are. The lower your level of self-awareness, the less aware you are of your ego, and this can result in you being enslaved by your ego. An ego exists solely for survival and is not concerned about your happiness or reality. People with high egos want to feel superior over others or feel the need to always be correct. People who love to complain may also have a big ego and use complaints to seek attention and validation from others. These are all the traits of a negative mindset that we have covered so far. Your ego is what defines your personal life story, along with how you identify with others. When your life doesn't follow how you expect your personal story to unfold, this can result in negative emotions. When you are able to identify your ego and change how you identify with others, you will then be able to feel more positive.

The nature of your emotions

Emotions are the most unpredictable aspects of our lives. You can be feeling happy today, and sad tomorrow. Because emotions are so unpredictable, they are nearly impossible to control. The only power you have is learning to control how you respond. To do this, you must be able to accept that emotions are transient. When you have a positive mindset, it will help you control your emotional responses.

Emotions and mindsets

I strongly encourage you to never blame yourself for any negative emotion that you experience. There is nothing wrong with you, and you are not mentally weak. Having negative emotions does not make you a bad person. Even if you are feeling sad or depressed today, it doesn't mean that you will never smile again. This is why having a positive mindset is so important for controlling your emotional responses. The golden rule you must remember is this: The manner in which you interpret your emotions is what will create suffering, and not the emotion itself. I want you to take this moment to reflect on some of the worst periods in your life, and the emotions that you felt during them. Maybe in those moments you felt as if you would escape the low that you felt. It was perhaps completely impossible to see yourself feeling happy once more. Even if you are presently going through that state, the good news is that by visualizing a happy future, you can overcome those negative emotions. It all comes back down to the power of your thoughts, thinking responsibly, and using the power of visualization.

Thoughts, visualization, and emotions

Your thoughts have the power to create and define your reality. This is why it is important that the quality of your thoughts be oriented toward what you would like to have in life, rather than channeled toward what you do not want. Your thoughts must consist of what you desire in life, rather than what you fear.

Changing and Controlling Your Emotions

The word "power" has been repeated multiple times throughout this book so far because that is what I want you to remember: You have the power to make the changes you want in your life. Just as you've come to realize that you have the power to change the quality of your thoughts, so, too, do you have the power to change and control your emotions. It also boils down to conditioning your mind to experience positive emotions rather than negative ones. Before you can learn how to control your emotions, it is useful to understand how your emotions are formed. With this knowledge in mind, we will move on to examining how to recognize when your emotions are controlling you. With awareness comes power and freedom, and then we take a closer look at how to let go of negative emotions, along with long-term techniques that you can use to control your emotions.

How Your Emotions Are Formed

Very few people actually know the process by which their emotions are formed. Even though emotions are something that we experience every day of our lives, most of us have never taken the time to gain a better understanding of those feelings and how they came about. Have you ever asked yourself, "Why am I feeling happy or sad, and what caused that feeling to occur?" This is the kind of question even I had never paid much attention to, not until I developed a deeper curiosity into understanding the power of our minds. Moving right along, what I came to learn—and what I will share with you, firstly—is that there are two different categories of negative emotions that you should be aware of. The first category entails spontaneous negative emotions. These occur without premeditation and depend on the external environment that triggered the emotional response. For instance, let's say you are terrified of snakes and encounter one in your home—that fear you feel in that moment is your spontaneous emotional response.

The next category of negative emotions includes the emotions you create mentally because of the nature of your thoughts. These emotions do not necessarily require an external situation to trigger a negative emotional response, and you may feel these emotions stronger and longer than the first category. Let us examine how this category works. The first part involves you randomly thinking of something, and your mind identifies with that thought. For instance, it is almost the end of the month, and you know that the rent will be due. You haven't had a stable job and are experiencing money issues. As you randomly think of your financial problems, anything related to money helps your mind to remain focused on the topic. The more you are able to identify with your thoughts, the more it creates an emotional response. Your emotions grow stronger the longer you think about the topic. In this example, the more you think about your financial problems, your worrying about those problems will intensify.

The reason why it is important to understand how these emotions are formed is because it helps to understand how you interpret issues, which in turn, develop your emotional response. If you repeatedly focus on your money, it makes it easier for thoughts related to your finances to occur. In other words, when you give negative thoughts the freedom to exist, they become your sole focus, and your emotional response to these thoughts increases. The key word in understanding how emotions are formed is "interpretation." Interpretation refers to how you make sense of your thoughts. Interpretation, combined with identification and thought repetition, is what leads to strong emotions being formed. When you are able to control one of these factors, or all of them, you will notice that you have greater control over your emotions. To summarize, for your negative emotions to increase in intensity and time span, you have to interpret your thoughts, then identify with those thoughts, and lastly, you must repeat these thoughts over and over again.

Now, let us take a closer look at these factors that control how your emotions are formed:

Interpretation: A proven fact is that people react differently to the same external scenario in completely different ways. This is because we interpret events differently. For instance, you may feel annoyed if your favorite restaurant got your lunch order wrong, whereas someone else may feel unaffected. A negative emotion will only arise after you have interpreted a specific situation. The actual scenario will not trigger your emotional response. This is your first step in learning how to regain control over your reality; when you learn how you interpret events that have occurred. Take, for example, if you were eagerly awaiting being promoted to a higher position at work but discovered that the promotion was given to another employee. Even though this may be disappointing, your reality will only remain upsetting if you interpret it as a negative and repeat the situation repeatedly in your mind. Your emotional response of disappointment, or maybe even anger, will grow into a core emotion because of how you interpreted the situation.

Identification: Your emotions can last for a longer time span because of how you identify with your thoughts. For your emotions to persist, you must give them all your attention, and that is how a negative emotion can become powerful. Many of us struggle to disengage from our emotions and believe that we are our emotions. This is incorrect, because as you have learned so far, emotions are temporary; they come, and they go. So, the more you think to yourself, "I am angry because I was skipped over for a promotion," or the more you believe you were not worthy of being promoted, this will result in how much more you identify with that emotion because you are giving it all your attention. The key is to remember that you are not an angry person. Rather, you are simply experiencing feelings of anger at that specific point in time. When you refuse to give any attention to any negative thoughts, you will notice that your negative emotions slowly begin to fade away. This is very critical, and I hope you can understand how much power you truly have in the process.

Repetition: As you have seen so far, the manner in which you interpret external situations, or your thoughts is what will determine your emotional response. You've also learned that the more attention you give to your thoughts and identifying with them, the more they translate into stronger emotions. Now, what can make negative emotions more powerful is when you constantly repeat negative thoughts, as you are conditioning your mind to always experience these emotions. For instance, in the example of being skipped for promotion; if you keep replaying the fact that you weren't promoted every day, your feelings of disappointment or anger will grow.

Signs your emotions are controlling you

We have covered quite a bit so far about emotions, and how they are formed. The overall goal is to learn how to exercise better control over your emotions. However, what if your situation is the complete opposite, and you are in fact being controlled by your emotions—how would you know? It is indeed quite possible for your emotions to control your behavioral response, and you may not even be aware that it is occurring. The following list provides some of the basic signs that may help you to identify if your emotions are indeed controlling you:

1. **You constantly feel the need to be busy:** One of the main signs that can indicate if your emotions are controlling you is your need to feel busy. If you are constantly occupied, you will likely be avoiding your thoughts and emotions. If you are experiencing any intense emotional discomfort, submerging yourself in your work can help you to avoid acknowledging your emotions.

2. **You judge yourself harshly because of your emotions:** The next sign is when you become your own worst critic and judge yourself for how you feel. We are all prone to feelings of anger, anxiety, or sadness. However, those who are controlled by their emotions judge themselves harshly for feeling these negative emotions. When you judge yourself over how you feel, you are actually creating more emotional distress for yourself.

3. **Procrastination is your friend:** Procrastination can be another sign that you are letting your emotions control you. Those who struggle with regulating their emotions also tend to become distracted easily and lose focus. This lack of focus may result in you not pursuing your goals or facing a situation that

you do not prefer because of the emotions you experience.

4. **You find it difficult to be alone:** People who are controlled by emotions actively avoid being alone, as alone time would require them to confront their emotions. This need to always interact with others is usually paired with the need to feel busy. The best way to avoid any negative emotions and to address how you feel would be to constantly surround yourself with the company of others.

5. **You avoid conflict at all costs:** Conflict or an argument with another person can be an uncomfortable situation that results in you feeling negative emotions. Whenever a conflicting situation occurs, there are usually associated feelings of irritability, fear, or anger, all of which you may want to completely avoid feeling.

6. **You feel irritated easily:** When you are unable to control your emotions, you are more prone to impulsive emotional outbursts, as

you may find yourself more easily triggered and irritated. Whenever there is an increase in negative emotional reactions and irritation, it could be a sign that your emotions have the upper hand over you.

7. **You are constantly overthinking:** As your emotions influence the way you think and feel about things, overthinking—which results in negative emotions such as stress, nervousness, or anxiety—can indicate that you are struggling to control your emotions.

The Power of Negative Thoughts and Emotions

Every once in a while, we are guaranteed to encounter an intense negative thought. Some of these thoughts we can ignore, however, there are some that will last longer, no matter how much we try to ignore them. The longer those negative thoughts last, the longer it will affect your mood and overall health. Negative thoughts have a special way of attacking your self-confidence and self-worth and can prevent you from interacting with others or completing daily tasks. Our minds are always thinking and engaging with our negative thoughts typically results in the production of negative emotions. It is often easier for our minds to focus more on the negative thoughts, rather than the positive ones. It is important for you to also learn the different types of negative thinking. The main ones include:

Reading minds: This category of negative thinking is characterized by your assumption of what others are thinking in relation to you. Say, for example, you call up your friend on the phone, and your call goes answered. However, instead of thinking that they may have a genuine reason as to why they were unable to answer your call, you automatically start thinking you did something that has upset your friend. This form of thinking can cause unnecessary damage to your relationships, as well as create anxiety that could've been avoided.

Guilty thoughts: Any time you notice that you've made a mistake and regret your course of action, thoughts of guilt are usually most present. Although you may have accepted that you are unable to change your past, it is easy to give in to feeling guilty at any point. The more you are unable to acknowledge your mistakes, the greater the negative feelings and thoughts of guilt you will have.

Telling your fortune: There are some people who automatically expect a negative outcome, regardless of the situation. This type of fortune telling is where you only think of the worst possible outcome that can occur. This negative type of mentality prevents you from being in control of your reality and enjoying being in the present moment, as you are always expecting a bad outcome at any given point. For instance, say you have an interview scheduled for a job you were highly anticipating, however, you keep telling yourself that you will fail the interview. Your reactions will be negative, as you are more likely to be nervous during the course of the interview, which in turn can ultimately result in your performance. Negative fortune telling is the polar opposite of the tool of creative visualization, as it lowers your self-confidence, and you only visualize the worst that can and will occur.

Letting go of negative emotions

So, we have covered how the process of interpreting, identifying, and repeating can result in the creation of emotions. The goal, then, is to learn how to use this process to create positive emotions, rather than negative emotions. Negative emotions prevent you from enjoying being present and having control over your reality. Of course, sometimes it may be difficult to avoid negative emotions altogether, which is why you need to learn how to let go of negative emotions that are keeping you back. Changing your perspective regarding your emotions is imperative in this instance. I want you to look at your emotions as energy that is constantly moving. Can you tell what happens when you stop that energy from being able to move freely? The end result is that energy accumulates. Far too many of us deal with our negative emotions by repressing those feelings, and consequently, we interrupt the flow of our emotions. Even though negative emotions can be intense, they are natural and should not be repressed. The more you repress your feelings, the more they will eventually become a part of your identity.

The last thing you want is to have emotional baggage that has developed over time, as this is what will prevent you from having complete control over your reality. To learn how to start letting go of any negative emotions that you might have allowed to build over time, you must observe your feelings while staying detached as much as possible. The next step is to label those emotions. Avoid making statements such as "I am hurt" or "I am angry," because these statements are how you identify with your emotions. The more accurate form of expressing yourself would be to say, "I feel hurt," as this gives the space needed to detach yourself from your feelings, rather than using them to describe who you are. The next step would be to question yourself as to why you are allowing yourself to feel this way. To truly be able to let go of any negative emotion, you need to establish if you are able to let this feeling go, and when.

Condition your mind

If you are unable to let how you feel go, the next best step would be to change your thinking. There is an old saying that suggests we become the product of our collective thoughts. Your thoughts and emotions are connected to each other. Your thoughts are what generate your emotions, and your emotions influence your actions. It all comes back to the original source of power: your mind. As human beings, we possess an incredible power—the power of imagination. We have the power to visualize what we want. In other words, we can turn the impossible into the possible. If you have a pessimistic outlook, you find it difficult to use your thoughts to manifest what you want in life. This is why you need to condition your mind through positive self-talk. Take the time to observe how you speak to yourself, and how it, in turn, influences the way you interpret and identify with your thoughts.

Emotional Intelligence

When you hear the words "emotional intelligence," what immediately comes to mind? Have you ever heard this term before? For some of us, emotional intelligence is a foreign concept and refers to our ability to monitor the emotions that we have, as well as being able to deal with the emotions of the people around us. In order to be perceived as emotionally intelligent, you must be able to tell the difference between the many types of emotions and be able to label them accurately. Once you are capable of that task, the next stage requires you to utilize the information you have gained in order to structure your behavioral responses, as well as influence how others feel and behave toward you. Emotional intelligence gives us the power to place ourselves in the shoes of the people we interact with, thereby creating more meaningful conversations, and having more control over our present lives. With this type of intelligence, you will notice that you have a deeper understanding of yourself, as well as stronger connections with people, and you will also feel happier, as you can make more productive decisions.

Emotional regulation and emotional intelligence

At one point or another, in all of our lives, we may notice that our emotions have begun to spin out of control. Whether it be as a result of an argument with someone, experiencing a personal failure or setback, or you are concerned about someone close to you, when you leave your emotions unchecked, they can ultimately lead to feelings of regret over things you said and did in the heat of the moment. What is even more critical to note is that it is not only your negative emotions that can result in harm or damage in a relationship—it is also your positive emotions, such as triumph or excitement, that are perceived as negative when used in the wrong context, unless you learn how to regulate those emotions.

What is emotional regulation?

Although it may sound to most people like a highly complex psychological skill, emotional regulation is actually a very simple mental process that most of us perform daily, either unconsciously or consciously. For example, after having an argument with a family member or friend, you may take a long walk, or listen to your favorite music to help you calm down. Or maybe you can work on controlling your laughter when a situation occurs that is unintentionally funny but requires a serious response. All of these are daily examples of how we regulate our emotions. Emotional regulation may also be extended to include the emotions of others around us, such as soothing your child when they are upset, or using constructive criticism when discussing a sensitive matter with another person.

The Selves: Self-Awareness, Self-Regulations, and Self-Motivation

So, why is emotional intelligence an important factor to discuss in relation to learning how to control your emotions? As we have seen thus far, you must be aware of how you interpret and identify with your thoughts. Your personality is responsible for your interpretation skills, and your personality is characterized by how you feel about yourself. Three components of emotional intelligence that help us to understand how we feel about who we are include self-awareness, self-regulation, and self-motivation.

Self-awareness: This component is regarded as the strongest aspect of emotional intelligence. This is where you conduct your own personal self-assessment that helps you to recognize all your strengths and weaknesses. You learn more about recognizing your emotions, and understand how they influence your behavior, as well as how they impact other people.

Self-regulation: This category refers to your ability to take control over your emotions and change how they will affect you. The best way to control your emotions is for you to practice being honest and maintaining your integrity in everything you do, as well as always accepting responsibility for your actions as an individual. Self-regulation requires you to be mindful regarding changes that will always occur, and to be flexible when professional or personal changes are required.

Self-motivation: As the term "self-motivation" suggests, you must be motivated to be a better person, and work on understanding your emotions. Emotional intelligence requires you to set a standard for yourself and be committed toward achieving that standard.

Long-Term Techniques to Help Control Your Emotions

In this section, I will discuss some techniques that will help you learn to control your emotions more efficiently over time.

Analyzing your negative emotions

- You can begin by making a list of the reasons as to why you may be experiencing these emotions. Try to evaluate your assumptions and stereotypes that may contribute to how you interpret the events that have happened.

- You can practice writing down how you feel every day in a journal. Use your journal to observe any recurring thought patterns. You can also use your journal to record visuals or affirmations that will help you to stay positive and overcome any negative emotions.
- The next technique you should learn is how to be mindful. Take the time to enjoy being present and observe your thoughts as situations occur. Daily meditation is a useful way of observing your emotions.

Moving away from sources of negativity

- After you have analyzed the nature of your negative emotions, make the effort to remove yourself from any external negative factors. If the environment you are situated in is negative, then move to a different location, or avoid spending time with negative people.
- You should also stop engaging in activities that are counterproductive, and do not have any positive influence over your reality.

Key Points to Remember From Chapter 5!

Although life can be a difficult journey at times, it is your ability to control your thoughts and emotions that will determine and shape your reality. Learning to control how you respond emotionally to your circumstances requires practice and patience. No one, myself included, is immune to the unpredictability of emotions. However, you have the power to use your emotions as a powerful tool. To recap, I want you to keep the following points in mind:

- Emotions are temporary. You must not allow yourself to become connected strongly with any negative emotion that you may experience. When you think responsibly and have a positive mindset, it will help you have much greater control over your emotional state.
- Emotions are a shared human experience, with the six basic types of emotions being happiness, sadness, anger, surprise, disgust, and fear. These emotions are influenced by our self-constructed egos, as well as how we identify with others.
- You can gain better control over your emotions when you are able to identify if your emotions are in fact controlling you, and how.
- You must analyze your environment and remove any negative elements in it, and condition your mind to let go of negative, counterproductive behavior.

Chapter 6: How to Be a Winner

Persistence is the quality of winners. Successful people never never give up.

—Lynda Field

I want you to stop for a moment and take a look around you. Think of the people who are successful and happy. Can you possibly identify what is the reason for their success? Consider the celebrities that you look up to as successful role models, as well. Do you know why they are so successful in life? It is very simple actually: They chose to view their world with a positive lens, rather than adopting a negative attitude. To be a winner, you must have a mindset that encourages and motivates you to succeed. Knowledge does not equate to success, but rather, having a mindset where you are committed to improving daily will help you to be a winner. I chose the words presented by Lynda Field for this chapter's epigraph, as they eloquently relate the attitude or mindset you need to be a winner; one of persistence. Why? Because people who are successful never give up. Winners have a specific type of mindset; a mindset known as a "growth mindset." So far, we have uncovered how our thoughts and emotions determine our reality. Now, it is time to address how your actions control your reality. In this chapter, you will learn more about growth mindsets, and how they help to create your label of success. We will also discuss what a fixed mindset is, how to change your mindset from fixed to growth, and ultimately, how to become a winner.

The Attitude of a Winner

One of the main reasons why I began my research on how to change your mindset is because over the years, I developed a keen interest in understanding how people manage after experiencing a setback or failure. What I discovered was that there are individuals who actually appreciate when they do fail at something. For them, their failure was a gift. I wondered what kind of mindset these people could have, that allowed them to view failure in such a positive light. These unique individuals at no time felt discouraged by their setback. In fact, they did not even feel as if they had failed. Instead, they never gave up, and tried once again. To them, failure was a form of learning, a form of growth. I also discovered that there are people who believe our human qualities are fixed or carved into our very being. These other people believe that failure means you are not smart, and that this can't be changed. In that moment, I realized that how you think has consequences, and dictates your actions. That is what led me to discover the two types of mindsets that determine who will be a winner in their life: a fixed mindset and a growth mindset.

Fixed Mindset Versus Growth Mindset

Depending on which view you have adopted for yourself, this is what will influence the manner in which you control your life. Your mindset will determine whether you are able to accomplish your goals, and when. The first type of mindset is a fixed mindset, in which you believe that your qualities are fixed and can't be changed. When you have a fixed mindset, you also feel the need to constantly prove yourself to others. A fixed mindset is usually developed from a very early age, as we are trained to believe that our human traits are carved into stone. For instance, if you received a failing grade on an exam, you were trained into thinking that you are not as smart as others, and that there is nothing you can do about it.

A growth mindset, on the other hand, is where you believe that your human qualities provide the starting point that you need in order to develop or grow as a person. With this type of mindset, people generally believe that with persistent effort, they can change and improve their qualities. Have you ever heard the saying that you can become anything you want if you put your mind to it? This type of mindset supports this saying, as there is the general consensus that a person's potential has not been fully revealed, and it is impossible and inaccurate to believe that one cannot be successful without making the effort first.

What type of mindset do you have?

Now that you have learned about the difference between a fixed and a growth mindset, are you able to identify which type of mindset you have? I want you to answer the following questions, keeping in mind that you should be completely honest with yourself as you answer. Your answers should help you to discover which category you fall under if you didn't already know. Read the following statements carefully and respond with either a "yes" or "no" as your answer.

1. I am capable of learning new things every day; however, this won't ultimately change my level of intelligence.
2. I believe that intelligence is a fixed characteristic about myself, and nothing will ever change that.

3. It is impossible for me to make changes in myself that would allow me to further myself.
4. I feel guilty about the mistakes I've made.
5. I believe that regardless of how intelligent I perceive myself to be, there is always room for growth.
6. I consider myself to be an optimistic person, and I believe that I have the potential to be successful.
7. I love learning new things, as they help me to improve my intelligence level.
8. I enjoy taking on new challenges that allow me to perform at my best.

If you answered "yes" to questions 1 to 4, then you most likely have a fixed mindset. Whereas, if you answered "yes" to questions 5 to 8, then you consider yourself as having a growth mindset. Mindsets, however, are not only based on your intelligence or abilities, as they are also about your personal qualities, as well. Read the following statements aloud, and then decide whether your answer is "yes" or "no" for each one.

1. I have a fixed personality. This will never change, and there is nothing I can do about it.
2. There are some skills that I can do differently, but the major aspects of who I am can't be changed.

3. Regardless of the type of personality I have, I have the power to change into a better person.

Which of the statements did you agree with the most? Questions 1 and 2 reflect a fixed mindset, whereas question 3 is the growth mindset question. Even if your answers reflect that of a fixed mindset, there is great news in store for you: You have the power to change your mindset.

Mastering a Winning Attitude

It is impossible to be a winner if you have a fixed mindset. This type of thinking only serves one purpose, and that is to limit your achievement. Your mind becomes filled with thoughts that interfere with your drive to become successful. The best way to become a winner is to master a winning or growth attitude. How can you achieve such a feat? It starts with the relationship that you build with yourself; after all, you need to believe in your capabilities before you can become a winner.

Your relationship with yourself is important

One thing that I truly believe in is that the secret to happiness can be found in nurturing healthy and meaningful relationships. Out of all the relationships we have, the most important relationship is the one that you build with yourself. Diane Von Furstenberg stated it perfectly when she said that "the most important relationship in your life is the relationship you have with yourself. Because no matter what happens, you will always be with yourself" (Crowley, 2021). It has been said that you will not be able to enjoy a happy and positive life if you have a negative mindset. Just the same, you can't develop the positive mindset that you need if you do not take the time to appreciate and acknowledge yourself as a person.

When you wake up every morning, what is the first thing that you say to yourself? What are some of the thoughts you have about yourself during the course of the day, or what do you tell yourself before you go to bed? Are your words negative or positive? Do your words empower you or leave you feeling disempowered? This is the truth that we have been analyzing over the last few chapters: The quality of your thoughts matters as they dictate how you feel about yourself. To become a winner, you must tell yourself that you have the power to become successful. A winning self-image all comes down to the power of positive self-talk. Self-talk is the factor that will define the type of relationship you build with yourself. Do you disrespect your own potential, or do you encourage and motivate yourself to succeed? It is your responsibility to take time every day to remind yourself that you can succeed.

You will notice that you become more successful when you nurture a loving relationship with yourself. Even when you don't have validation from others around you, it is important to have self-love. When you are able to practice appreciation and gratitude for who you are and everything in your life, it helps to nurture a more positive relationship with yourself, thereby helping you to build a positive mindset. To take the first step in building a better relationship with yourself, I want you to remind yourself of your awesomeness, and do not judge yourself.

Think winning thoughts

After you have taken the initiative to build a better relationship with yourself, it is important to take control of your thoughts. The power of visualization is also a great technique that winners use. I want you to stop right now and visualize yourself as the person you would like to be in the future. If your goal is to be the CEO of your own company, then visualize that you are that person. Winners know who they want to be, and they go after it. Negative thinking only hinders your success, as you are more likely to create excuses that deter your success. Even if you can possibly find 99 reasons as to why you won't be successful, you only need one reason to believe that you will accomplish it all. When you think winning thoughts, you inspire yourself to take on challenges. Your life and reality become a choice, and your choice is to be successful. A winning attitude will be the foundation of your success, and you have the power to control it simply by thinking positively.

Associate yourself with winners

If you truly want to be a winner, then you have to associate yourself with like-minded individuals who are already winners, or who also want to be a winner. You definitely should avoid people who have no direction or ambition. When you associate yourself with others who recognize their own purpose, this, in turn, fuels your desire to understand your own, as well. When you associate with others who share a similar vision to yours, the nature of your conversations will be different. People with a vision of success do not spend time complaining or dwelling on their failures and mistakes. Instead, they are discussing their dreams and goals, and what strategies they can use to accomplish all of them. They do not seek validation from others, but uplift themselves instead, and are focused on finding solutions to their problems, rather than dwelling on the issues they face.

What I am discussing here with you is that you must choose where and who to invest your energy and time into. Your friends are a strong reflection of who you are, and the values that you believe in. How do you plan on being a winner if you associate yourself with people who are afraid of being successful? Let me ask you a critical question: Have you ever taken the time to analyze the people who you spend the most amount of time with? Think about it; when you are around someone frequently, you begin to adopt similar mannerisms to them. In time, you can become more like the people you associate with, and you don't even realize when it occurs. So, let's say your best friend is someone with a pessimistic and negative attitude, who constantly complains, and believes that these qualities of theirs are fixed, and that there is no room for success. Can you see how being around such negative energy constantly can eventually transfer over to you?

When you make the decision to avoid spending all your time with negative thinkers, or people who do not contribute to your happiness and goals— although it can be uncomfortable at first—in the long run, it can completely transform your entire life. People who are motivated to be winners help to support others to succeed. They can provide you with constructive feedback and remind you of the goals that you desire. A winner must choose to surround themselves with others who inspire the positive change that they want in their life.

Be your greatest fan

The honest truth is that there is absolutely no one else like you. Have you ever stopped to wonder how others look at you? Are you able to see just how wonderful and deserving you truly are? You have to be your biggest supporter and believe that you were made to accomplish great things. Sometimes it can be hard to truly recognize the awesome qualities that we possess. Even I am confident enough to admit that at times, I am not always my own biggest fan. Even in preparing this book, I was extremely hard on myself at various moments. In fact, writing this book has helped me to become better at being my own personal cheerleader. What I learned in writing this book was to set aside time to celebrate my accomplishments in my life. My success started when I took the time to believe in who I am, and what I can accomplish. To become your own fan, you have to take time to congratulate yourself for overcoming anything that you have struggled with; you have to talk to yourself as if you are already a winner.

From Failure to Winning: The Story of Stephen

King

I have always believed in the power of inspiration, and one of the best ways to inspire yourself is to hear about the success stories of others who we look up to as role models. Celebrities are always in the spotlight for their personal lives, but rarely do we realize that they face all the same challenges we do. Have you ever heard of Stephen King? If you are a fan of reading horror books like me, then you can most definitely recognize Stephen King as one of the world's best-selling authors, with over 85 books published. Perhaps you've read or seen the movie *It*, featuring Pennywise the Clown, and you were terrified for nights afterward, much like myself. If this has happened to you, then you are certainly familiar with the wonderful work of Stephen King. His journey and success as an author completely personifies why you must not let failure define you, but rather, you must use your rejection as a starting point to become a winner.

Stephen King did not become a success overnight, in fact, he encountered multiple rejections and hardship on his journey. What set him apart from other authors, was the fact that he never gave up. He had a goal of becoming a successful author, and he kept moving forward to achieve his goal. From a young age, he had to work multiple jobs and deal with financial issues that prevented him from writing. He was even unable to purchase his first typewriter, which led to him borrowing one to use from his wife. He explained in various interviews that his emotions sometimes controlled him, and he felt like giving up. At one point, he had crumpled up a bunch of his work and tossed it in the trash. His wife, who had become his biggest fan and supporter, saved those pages from the garbage, thankfully, and encouraged him to keep writing.

This was his defining moment, and he dedicated himself to writing his first manuscript, entitled *Carrie*. He visualized that his novel would be his first success and continued to work hard despite multiple rejections from publishing companies. A small publishing firm made the offer to publish *Carrie*, however, and it went on to sell more than a million copies worldwide in the first year of being released. As you can definitely see from the success story of Stephen King, having a goal and believing in change, regardless of the obstacles you face, provides the foundation that you need in order to become a winner. You simply cannot let your fear of failure or being rejected hold you back from potential success. Choose people who can become your support system and who will motivate you to stay persistent throughout your journey.

Self-Discipline and Investing in Yourself

Becoming a winner at anything you put your mind to requires motivation. You can't make it to the top if you are lazy and unmotivated; no one ever has. When a winner has a goal in mind, it requires self-discipline and excellence-oriented behavior. Whether it is in sports, or being more successful at work, your dedication and desire to succeed are what will help you to establish yourself. The best combination that a winner can have is a growth mindset paired with self-discipline, as where these two things meet is where success begins. You may be asking at this point, "what is self-discipline all about?" Although there are various perspectives on what self-discipline is, what I learned is that the more disciplined you are, the more control you have over your life. A clear definition of self-disciple states that it is "the ability to suppress prepotent responses in the service of a higher goal, and such a choice is not automatic but rather requires conscious effort" (Duckworth & Seligman, 2006). As you can see from this definition, it is all about making the effort to achieve your goals and staying committed to the task.

In combination with self-discipline, you must also invest in yourself. You have to decide that you want to be a winner at all costs. When you think of people who are winners or are successful, do you know what made them this way, as opposed to those who never made it? It is because they invested in themselves. One of the best investments that a person can make is to invest in themselves. A winner must be strategic about their investment, but it must also be intentional. What does this even mean? Well, you need to make time every day to plan how you intend on achieving your goals. How often do you set aside time to reflect on what you did on a given day, and what can you do the following day to improve yourself? If you set aside even 15 minutes out of each day, you are taking the time to invest and plan your strategy of success. Success does not simply come to you; you must plan how you want to win.

Habits of winners

Your self-discipline is revealed by the habits that you practice daily. When you allow negative habits to take control, they will prevent you from being the winner you are capable of becoming. Your habits are what determine your reality. If you want to be a winner, there are different positive habits that you can incorporate into your life to help you along the way.

1. **Start small:** Even though you may be motivated to win, you can actually impede

your own success by trying to accomplish too much at once. For instance, let's say your goal is to lose weight and stay healthy. It would be detrimental to your health if you were to go to the gym every day of the week, and drastically change your diet in a short space of time. When you set unrealistic goals for yourself, the process of being successful can become overwhelming. The best approach for you is to set smaller, more realistic goals.

2. **Create a routine:** All winners have one thing in common, and that is that they created a daily routine for themselves. When you get up each day, do you know what your action plan for that day is? Using the same example of having a goal to lose weight, if you were to create a routine of going to the gym twice a week, and you stay committed to that routine, you would notice how much smoother your gym day would run as time went on. Winning is accomplished faster and easier when you can create a routine that outlines when and how you plan to accomplish your goals.

3. **Write down your progress:** We all feel wonderful when we have accomplished something that we truly desired. A true winner does not only acknowledge the big wins, but takes the time to celebrate the smaller victories, as well. Every day, we all

achieve small victories, but how many of us take the time to reflect on the smaller accomplishments? When you are able to reflect on everything you have achieved, it helps you feel motivated enough to continue staying on course. This is why you should develop the habit of writing down all your daily accomplishments and making daily self-reflection a part of your routine. Reflecting on your accomplishments functions as a form of positive reinforcement that we all need to feel further motivated.

Abundance and winning

Part of developing a winning attitude is understanding the importance of abundance. You are not the person who wants to succeed, but you are also not in direct competition with anyone. Thinking abundantly allows us to realize that everyone can be a winner, because there are enough resources to share among us all. The opposite of thinking abundantly is when you have a mindset of scarcity. Stinson (2019) clarifies that an abundance mindset is "a concept in which a person believes there are enough resources and successes to share with others." Stinson (2019) then explains that "the scarcity mindset (i.e., destructive, and unnecessary competition) [...] is founded on the idea that, if someone else wins or is successful in a situation, that means you lose; not considering the possibility of all parties winning (in some way or another) in a given situation."

How do you know if you have a mindset of abundance? Think about how you look at the world around you. Do you feel threatened when others are successful? The greatest aspect of thinking with abundance is that "when you feel abundant, you experience more gratitude, appreciation, and feel more positive about yourself. With an abundance mentality you focus on the unlimited opportunities available for positive growth and development" (Pettit, 2018).

Developing a mindset of abundance

If you make it a point to think abundantly, you will also notice that you feel confident and more grateful about your life. This form of thinking helps you to remain focused on what you have already accomplished, as well as future opportunities that are in store for you. Abundance thinking also helps you to create better goals for your life. Thinking abundantly is all about your attitude; an attitude which helps you to visualize bigger, and take the action required to achieve your vision. Having an abundance mindset allows you to:

- Grow as a person without any limitations.

- View your reality as being blessed with opportunities.
- Be grateful, regardless of your circumstances.
- Feel inspired, creative, and grow faster.

Here are some steps that you can follow to help you develop an attitude of abundance:

Focus on being grateful about what you already have: True winners are grateful for all their accomplishments, and don't envy what others have achieved. When you think abundantly, you are too happy with all that you have and who you are.

Focus on your winning strengths: With an abundance mindset, your weaknesses pale in comparison to your strengths. Your unique strengths help you to feel more confident and realize that anything is possible.

Closing thoughts

No matter how difficult the journey may be, a winner is a person who is focused on accomplishing all their goals. A winner believes in themselves and is prepared to face all challenges that can arise, as well as any obstacles that can obstruct how they achieve what they want in life. We are not all born with skills and talents that can't be changed, but we can develop our skill sets and master them over time. When you think of successful athletes such Michael Jordan or

Serena Williams, do you know what made them winners? Their perseverance. A winner does not quit, even when they have encountered setbacks. Famous scientists such as Isaac Newton and Albert Einstein certainly did not give up from accomplishing their visions, even when some of their initial theories and experiments were viewed as failures. This is what will separate you as a winner from everyone else: your determination. You can only be determined if you have the right attitude.

Key Points to Remember From Chapter 6!

Now, let us recap the major points from this chapter that you must keep in mind if you want to become a winner:

- If you want to be a winner, you must have a winning attitude, otherwise known as a growth mindset.
- As a winner, you must believe in the power of change, perseverance, and never giving up, despite the obstacles or challenges you may encounter.
- Winners all have one trait in common: They view failure as an opportunity to learn, rather than a setback in their lives. Failure opens the pathway to growth and success.
- There are two types of mindsets that control your outlook and will determine your level of

success. These are a fixed mindset and a growth mindset.

- With a fixed mindset, you believe that your human characteristics, as well as your external surroundings are fixed, or can't be changed, no matter how much you try. Whereas with a growth mindset, your personal qualities and external environment provide the foundation and starting point that you need to develop as a person.

- To begin transforming your attitude into a winning attitude, you must develop a loving and healthy relationship with yourself and become your greatest fan. You must also think winning thoughts and choose to associate yourself with winners.

- Understanding the role of self-discipline and investing in yourself is key to becoming a winner.

- A winner also has a mindset of abundance as opposed to scarcity, as you believe that there are more than enough resources for everyone to share and be successful.

Chapter 7: Taking Back Control of Your Reality

You are in control of your life. Don't ever forget that. You are what you are because of the conscious and subconscious choices you have made.

—Barbara Hall

You have now reached the most important and exciting part of your journey, and you are ready to use all that you have learned to take back control of your reality. I have shown you the importance of changing the quality of your thoughts, as well as controlling your emotions. This is because you can lose control over your own reality when you are not aware of your internal power. Your reality is what you design it to be. Read over the words written by Barbara Hall up above; what stands out to you about them? For me, it is the very first line, because yes—I am in control of my own life. We all are. Our decisions determine who we become. This is why I encouraged you to challenge yourself to think more responsibly. You may be wondering now, what else can you do to take back control of your reality? Well, in this chapter, I want to discuss the importance of having the right attitude. A positive thinker must have an attitude that aligns with their thoughts. I've mentioned the word "goals" before, but in this chapter, we will go into more detail about how goals help you to control where you want your life to head. Lastly, you will learn how to empower yourself, and set the tone for personal growth.

It All Starts With Your Attitude

Do you know the one factor that defines everything that occurs in your life? It is your attitude. If you were to meet someone tomorrow who has no idea how to captivate their audience's attention, or if you met someone who is constantly bitter and negative, you would find that their behavior has everything to do with their attitude. A positive attitude equates to a happy life. It is a proven fact that great things occur for good people, and when you have a positive attitude, great things will fall into place for you, as well. Your attitude, just like every other character trait we have discussed, can be changed. Our attitudes develop during our childhood and grow as we transition into adults. So, even though there are some who may believe that they can't change their attitude, that is definitely inaccurate.

Feeling Out of Control

When you have a negative attitude, it can result in you feeling as if your life is spiraling, and you are no longer in control of what happens to you. But what led to you feeling this way? Perhaps you feel as if you do not have enough time, emotional support from others, or finances. You may even believe that your life is out of your control simply because you lack direction and a sense of purpose. This is why it is important to understand your attitude. When you do, I can assure you that life as you know it will never be the same again. So, here is my question: If you do not take control over your own life, then who will? What will you allow to influence you, or direct your future? I hope you looked at yourself, and answered, "me." It all begins with changing the attitude you have about your life.

How to Change Your Attitude

A positive attitude will always remain as the key to improving your life and taking control over your reality. Let us explore some ways that you begin to change your attitude:

Appreciate Life: As human beings, we all face situations or circumstances in our lives that can take a mental, emotional, and even physical toll on us every day. Too many times, we allow the negative situations that we encounter to get the better of us, and as a result, our mindset and attitudes can become disoriented. Whenever you are faced with a difficult situation, you should take a moment to reflect on other positive things that have occurred before, and how happy they made you feel. The best way to overcome a difficult situation is to shift our focus back to the positive aspects of our lives and acknowledge the accomplishments we have made so far.

Guard and Feed Your Mind: Your mind is the most powerful resource that you own, so you should be mindful of the different factors that can influence it. You should eliminate negative external factors that do not help you to grow as a person. Furthermore, try to treat your mind as you do your body, and only feed it information that is inspirational and motivational. What you feed your mind will influence your thoughts, emotions, and attitudes.

Watch Your Language: Your words have power, so you need to be careful and choose positive rather than negative words. Your words can either tear you down or build you up as a person. They are how you reflect your thoughts, so try changing your speech to be more uplifting, and you will surely notice a shift in your attitude.

Creating Your Best Life With Goals

The best way to enjoy life is when you can be successful without limitations. Are you interested in living your best life possible? I am assuming your answer is "yes," since you have made it this far into this book. Goals are your personal tool of structuring life and taking back control over your destination. Creating a goal helps to give your future a perspective, as you have established what you would like to achieve, and when. This is what will separate you from others who feel as if they have no control over their reality, because they have not created any goals, or are at least undetermined to pursue their goals.

Types of Goals

Let us look briefly at some of the various types of goals you can have for your life:

- Relationship goals
- Educational goals

- Health goals
- Financial goals
- Individual development goals
- Spiritual goals

Setting the goals you need

In order for your goal setting objectives to be successful, you must believe in the process first. When you doubt your ability to completely transform your life via goals, then you have undermined the process of taking control of your life. Everything you do revolves around the power of your thoughts, and it starts with believing that creating goals will help you to get what you want. When you believe in what you are doing, your beliefs will transform into action. After believing in your goals, you have to use the technique of visualization to create a mental image of what you want to have happen. If your goal is to start your own company in two years, then you need to visualize the route you must take to make that goal happen. Try to make your visual as clear as possible, as it will increase the likelihood of it happening.

Your Future Is Your Destination

I want you to strive to always be better than how you were the day before. I also encourage you to continue making steps toward living an authentic life. Even though you may feel terrified of what might be next, your future can appear less scary, simply because you have mastered the skill of thinking positively. You need to recognize that your past has nothing to offer you—instead, understand that your future is your destination. To take control of your reality requires you to live in the moment of where you are at, right now. Live your dreams without fear, and do not worry about what is yet to come. You may not be able to control what happens next, but you can control how you respond. So, how do you recognize when you are truly ready to control your reality? I will discuss some characteristics of growth that will reflect if you are ready to be the master of your own universe.

Signs You Are Ready to Control Your Reality

You know you are ready to control your reality because you recognize just how simple and easy going your life has become because of the changes you have made to your thoughts and outlook. Your life has changed to one of creation and power, all because of your mindset. The most important sign that shows you that you're ready is your ability to overcome the following bad habits: lack of vision and lack of accountability.

Avoiding a Lack of Vision

Whenever you experience a lack of results, it is usually because there was no action. If you truly want to take control, you must know what you want and how you can actualize your dreams. When you avoid being the type of person who doesn't have a blueprint or vision for their life, it is the first sign that you are ready to achieve your fullest potential. Your life is whatever you choose it to be, so you must be deliberate about your vision. Consistency should always be your best friend, as to accomplish your vision requires persistence and focus.

Be accountable

You must hold yourself accountable for all of your actions at all times. The only person who can be held responsible for you is you, and nobody else. Your performance and the relationship you have with yourself will drastically improve when you are able to take full and complete responsibility over every decision that you make. It will help others to respect you, and even more importantly, it will help you begin to respect yourself. How does this help you to take control of your reality, exactly? Firstly, it shows that you know what needs to be done in your life, and you are not going to complain or blame others when things do not work out as planned. A positive mindset requires accountability. It gives you the power to make the choices you must make, to set your goals, and to understand that this is your life—and no one else's.

Empower Yourself

You might have heard the term "self-empowerment" before, but have you ever really stopped to assess what the term means? Self-empowerment is characterized by your ability to make the conscious decision to take control of your reality. It includes making positive decisions, advancing yourself by action, and being confident in your skill of creating and achieving your goals. Self-empowerment is how you recognize your strength and your role in being the master of your reality. When you feel self-empowered, it is because you have recognized what your strengths and weaknesses are, and you are motivated to achieve more in your life. Self-empowerment also means that you are confident enough to ask for help along the path of your journey, as it helps you to become a stronger person.

For me, my self-empowerment grew out of my determination to succeed and achieve more in my life. I was determined to achieve things that I never thought possible. I was determined to publish my own book and share my knowledge with others. I created my goal, and I visualized what I wanted in my future. The fact that you are reading this book is solid proof of the power of visualization and setting goals. You can also enjoy the same level of success and feel in control of the direction that your life is heading. Everything that we have discussed in this book so far may seem daunting and challenging to put into action in your own life, but it is actually quite easy. What you need to do is be patient with yourself as you slowly implement new habits into your daily agenda. The following are some steps that you can adapt into your daily regime in order to help you feel self-empowered:

Self-empowerment steps

1. Do not take your positive mindset for granted. In almost every chapter, we have seen the words "positive mindset" repeatedly, because that is how powerful your mind is. All of the strategies that we have discussed in each chapter have required you to think positively, and to practice engaging in positive self-talk. The only way you can understand your role in

shaping your life is if you love yourself and accept responsibility over your life.

2. "Owning your words" simply means to say what you mean and mean what you say. Be comfortable saying "no" when you do not want to do something and take responsibility for how you make others feel through your words.

3. Self-care is the foundation of self-empowerment. You must be kind to yourself, and overall, be patient with your growth. The better you feel both mentally and physically, the easier it will be for you to get up and get things done in your life. Taking care of yourself can also help you to be exposed to more possibilities. When you present the version of yourself you are striving to be, the world notices. You must also trust in your skills, and never doubt your capabilities, as you have all the tools needed to be successful.

Self-empowerment is not a trait that we are born with; it is a learned skill. An empowered person respects themselves, accepts their insecurities, and does not let their doubts cloud their outlook on life. The mindset of a self-empowered person is never pessimistic, but rather, it is strong and determined. When you feel self-empowered, it leads to overall personal growth.

Personal Growth

When you hear the words "personal growth," what do they mean to you? Have you ever assessed just how much you have grown as a person over the last few months, or even the last few years of your life? Personal growth can be viewed as "a process of spiritual, physical, social, and spiritual growth that lasts a lifetime. It is a process of active learning and developing new skills long after formal education has been completed" (Ashiq, 2020). What makes personal growth so crucial to taking control of your reality, is the number of possibilities that it creates. When you grow as a person, your life and the opportunities afforded you expand. However, for personal growth to be successful as a tool, it requires your complete involvement. You must be motivated and desire to see an improvement in your life. The comfort zone that you have been living in must cease to exist, and you must have an open mind to learn new things. Personal growth requires you to be open to change, as your reality is not fixed—in fact, it can grow and improve.

Be open to change

For personal growth to occur, you must have a growth mindset, which I introduced to you earlier on in Chapter 6. A growth mindset is characterized by the belief that people can change. When you have a growth mindset, you are actively looking for ways to learn. You may find yourself asking questions such as, "Is there anything that I can learn from what occurred?" or "What can I do to improve?" When you are open to change, it gives you even more courage to pursue your dreams and goals. Most importantly, change helps you learn successful ways of making your dreams your reality. "Is change hard?", you may also ask. Well, it may sound complicated, but it is actually simpler than you even realize. Just by learning about the types of mindsets and identifying your own, you are motivating yourself to make a change.

I once had a conversation with a close friend who was in college and preparing to submit their final year thesis for their undergraduate degree. She explained to me how she had submitted her research to an academic journal for review, in hopes that her work would be published in their monthly journal. However, when she received feedback, she was completely devastated by the feedback she received. She felt as if both her academic work, and who she was as a person, had been judged. Although there was a request for minor changes, she felt demotivated, and could not complete the changes requested. She felt as if making any amendments would be pointless and wouldn't change their decision. Can you guess why I shared this story with you? I want you to observe, through consideration of my friend's story, how having a fixed mindset and not being open to change affects your reality. My friend's negative thinking kept her from making the changes she needed in order to achieve the goal she had set for herself. She may not have been able to control what happened, but she had the power to choose how she responded. Using what you know and have learned so far, what advice would you have given in this situation?

Answer personal growth questions

I understand that for some, it may not be completely easy to let go of a belief that has become a part of who you are and has played a role in creating your ego and self-esteem. It may feel even more daunting to accept a mindset that encourages you to embrace things that might have made you feel insecure or threatened, such as criticism, challenges, or setbacks. Even when I was in the process of changing my mindset to one of growth, I felt uncertain at times. What I chose to do was record my progress and list my successes daily. At the end of each day, I was able to review my results and see how many changes I had made, and it felt satisfying. You have to be willing to open yourself up to change and growth. Only you can set the tone and direction for your personal growth.

The rest is entirely up to you. I want to leave you with three questions to kickstart your journey toward personal improvement. Those questions are:

1. What will you start doing differently in your life?
2. What things will you stop doing completely?
3. What things will you continue to do?

These questions will help you to identify what you need to do to achieve your vision, what factors you must eliminate, and what you are already doing that is making a difference and should thus continue.

Key Points to Remember From Chapter 7!

We covered a lot of ground in this final chapter, and I want you to always remember that the power of controlling your reality resides within you. As we come to a close, I want you to reflect on the major themes that you learned in this chapter:

- Taking back control of your reality must first begin with you realizing that you are the only person in control of your life.
- Your thoughts, emotions, and all of the decisions that you have made—whether consciously or subconsciously—have all contributed to the person that you have

become, and help to design the reality you live in.

- The type of attitude you have defines and controls what you will experience in your life. You can choose to have a negative attitude or a positive attitude.
- Your attitude, however, is not fixed, and can be changed from a negative to a positive one, if you practice appreciating your life for what it is, as well as guarding and feeding your mind, and paying attention to the words you speak to yourself and others.
- You can create your best life by creating goals for yourself. Goals give your reality perspective and a sense of direction. You must visualize your goals clearly for them to take effect.
- You are ready to control your reality when you can avoid having a lack of vision or inconsistency, as well as if you can hold yourself accountable for all of your actions.
- Self-empowerment provides the skills and determination that you will need to make the best decisions in order to take complete control over your reality.
- You must believe in personal growth, as this will motivate you to improve and control the direction toward which your life is headed. You must be open to accepting change and

should be able to set the tone for growth by answering what you will do differently, what you will start doing, and what you will continue to do in your life.

Conclusion

Instead of worrying about what you cannot control, shift your energy to what you can create.

—Roy T. Bennett

For many of us, it may be very tempting to believe that change is impossible. However, change is surely on its way, and it began the moment you opened this book. I truly hope that after reading all the information I have provided for you in these pages, that you've come to witness and understand the incredible power of your mind. I know change can be very tough, but in the end, the majority of people all admit that it was worth it. When you are able to see how much your life can be enhanced, then this process of growth is definitely worth it. Why? Because you would get to experience all the positive things you didn't have before and feel much better about yourself in a way you wouldn't have felt if you hadn't changed your mindset.

A New Way Forward

The very last thing I want for you to experience is to one day get up out of your bed and realize that you hate the life you are living, or what you do for a living. As you've grown older in your life, you probably look back, and consider that you did the things you were supposed to do; you went to school and looked for a job. You pursued a life that is stable, but fixed, and you believed that this was how your life was meant to be. Over time, though, you have allowed too many factors to make decisions for the outcome of your life, which have resulted in you forging a life that you do not truly want to live. This book was meant to be your personal reminder that you are the driver of your life, and only you can—and should—be in the driver's seat. It is time for you to realize that maybe all along you've been stuck in a negative and fixed mindset. You can manifest the reality you always dreamed of by changing how you view yourself and your surroundings. Let's quickly review the key ways to change your mindset, in order to help you live a more positive life. In this book, you learned that complaining is characteristic of a negative mindset, and leaves you stuck in your situation, rather than fixing the problem. The best way to overcome a negative mindset is to engage in positive self-talk. Self-validation is one of the first means in which you can transition into a positive outlook, as the best form of validation always comes from within ourselves. We learned that it is our responsibility to think positively and learning how we interpret the events that happen around us will help to determine our reality. This reality is controlled by the nature of our thoughts, our actions, and our emotions. As such, we also discussed what emotions are, and the various means by which you can learn to regulate and control your emotions. Overall, we discussed the essence of a growth mindset, and how to change from a fixed mindset to a growth mindset, in order to be a winner and take back control over your reality. I am glad that you now have a deeper understanding of what is required to be successful and happy. Once you have a dream or goal for your life, now is the time to start. It was your decision to start this journey toward changing your mindset, and I am positive that with the knowledge you have newly acquired, you will be able to achieve a positive new beginning. Congratulations on the start of a beautiful journey!I want you to remember all the lessons that you've learned, and to apply them to your life. Your life will always be the manifestation of all your goals and thoughts. When you develop a negative way of thinking, then you will ultimately view the world negatively. This is your chance to master your mindset. Your attitude can be your superpower if you take control of your mind. I want you to get up every day, and tell your brain, "Yes, I can." These are all the lessons we've covered in learning how to change your mindset, and ultimately shift your reality. They are your tools for success. No matter what challenge you face, keep on going. You now have everything you will ever need, and it is all within you.

Next Steps

I wanted to bring this book to a close by leaving you with one final quote that was stated in the epigraph for this section. In it, Roy Bennet explains that you should never worry about the things that you cannot control. Instead, you should focus your energy on what you can create in your life. This is what this entire book was all about. You may not be able to control the circumstances or situations you find yourself in, but you are in control of how you respond. Will changing from a fixed to a growth mindset solve every problem you face? The answer is no. However, I am confident that you will be able to live a richer, happier, and more successful life because of your mindset. This is the time for you to decide how to start that change. Your mindset will always be available to you, helping you to create a path into your winning future.

Your future self will thank you for staying committed to your journey.

References

50 Best Winning Quotes To Take You To The Top. (2021, September 6). Kidadl.com. https://kidadl.com/quotes/best-winning-quotes-to-take-you-to-the-top#famous-quotes-about-winning

60 Responsibility Quotes - Inspirational Words of Wisdom. (n.d.). Www.wow4u.com. https://www.wow4u.com/responsibility-quotes/

A quote by Lao Tzu. (n.d.). Www.goodreads.com. https://www.goodreads.com/quotes/8203490-watch-your-thoughts-they-become-your-words-watch-your-words

Ashiq, F. (2020, April 8). *Personal Growth: A Definite Guide To Self Growth - Thrive.* https://thriveglobal.com/stories/personal-growth-a-definite-guide-to-self-growth/amp/

Cherry, K. (2013, August 2). *Emotions and Types of Emotional Responses*. Verywell Mind; Verywellmind. https://www.verywellmind.com/what-are-emotions-2795178

Cherry, K. (2021, February 20). *The Big Five Personality Traits*. Verywell Mind. https://www.verywellmind.com/the-big-five-personality-dimensions-2795422

Crowley, K. (2021, February 8). *7 Ways to Fall in Love With Yourself This Valentine's Day Regardless of Your Relationship Status - Gymondo® Magazine: Fitness, Nutrition & Weight Loss*. https://www.gymondo.com/magazin/en/motivation-en/7-ways-to-fall-in-love-with-yourself-this-valentines-day-regardless-of-your-relationship-status

Crum, A. J., Salovey, P., & Achor, S. (2013). Rethinking stress: The role of mindsets in determining the stress response. *Journal of Personality and Social Psychology, 104*(4), 716–733. https://doi.org/10.1037/a0031201

Dr. Charles Stangor. (2014). Principles of Social Psychology - 1st International Edition. In *Opentextbc.ca.* BCcampus. https://opentextbc.ca/socialpsychology/

Hall, K. (2012, February 3). *What is Validation and Why Do I Need to Know?* Psych Central. https://psychcentral.com/blog/emotionally-sensitive/2012/02/levels-of-validation#3

Hoffman, J. (2019, January 8). *Why Jim Carrey Wrote Himself a $10-Million Check Before He Had $10 Million.* Medium. https://socialmediajosh.medium.com/why-jim-carrey-wrote-himself-a-10-million-check-before-he-had-10-million-3618090c9e

Ishiyama, F. I. (1993). On Self-Validation. *The Trumpeter*, *10*(4). https://trumpeter.athabascau.ca/index.php/trumpet/article/view/365/574

Jameson, R. (2014, April 28). *Be Careful of Your Thoughts: They Control Your Destiny*. HuffPost. https://www.huffpost.com/entry/be-careful-of-your-though_b_5214689/amp

Jane. (2016). *5 Reasons Why People Complain*. Habitsforwellbeing.com. https://www.habitsforwellbeing.com/5-reasons-why-people-complain/

LCMHCS, H. M. (2021, October 23). *Like yourself more: the power of self-validation*. McKenzieCounseling.

https://www.mckenziecounseling.org/post/the-power-of-self-validation

leadingpersonality. (2013, March 15). *What is Positive Thinking?* Leading Personality. https://leadingpersonality.wordpress.com/2013/03/15/what-is-positive-thinking/amp/

linaberezovska. (2018, December 26). *Quotes About Controlling Emotions: A Good Way to Inner Peace.* EnkiQuotes. https://www.enkiquotes.com/quotes-about-controlling-emotions.html

Martin, S. C. (2019). *The CBT workbook for perfectionism : evidence-based skills to help you let go of self-criticism, build self-esteem, & find balance*. New Harbinger Publications.

Meah, A. (2017, April 25). *30 Inspirational Quotes On Taking Control Of Your Life | AwakenTheGreatnessWithin.*

https://www.awakenthegreatnesswithin.com/30
-inspirational-quotes-on-taking-control-of-your-
life/

Meah, A. (2018, January 14). *35 Inspirational
Quotes To Stop You From Complaining |
AwakenTheGreatnessWithin.*
https://www.awakenthegreatnesswithin.com/35
-inspirational-quotes-to-stop-you-from-
complaining/

Morrison-Brandauer, S. (2014, April 9). *Show me
your friends and I will tell you who you are...Of
Journeys and Roots.* http://www.of-journeys-
and-roots.com/2014/04/09/show-me-your-
friends-and-i-will-tell-you-who-you-are/

Pettit, M. (2018, December 6). *7 Ways to Develop
an Abundance Mindset. Lucemi Consulting:
Strategic Business Coaching.*

https://lucemiconsulting.co.uk/abundance-mindset/

Positive Thinking Quotes (2948 quotes). (2019). Goodreads.com. https://www.goodreads.com/quotes/tag/positive-thinking

Sasson, R. (n.d.). *What is Positive Thinking and Why You Need It.* https://www.successconsciousness.com/blog/positive-attitude/what-is-positive-thinking/

Scott, E. (2022, March 25). *Stop Complaining to Have a More Positive Life.* Verywell Mind. https://www.verywellmind.com/how-and-why-stop-complaining-3144882

Stevens, T. G. (2010). *You can choose to be happy : "rise above" anxiety, anger, and depression, with research evidence.* Wheeler-Sutton Pub. Co.

Stinson, N. (2019, August 16). *The Chopra Center.*
The   Chopra   Center.
https://chopra.com/articles/10-steps-to-develop-an-abundance-mindset

Validation   Quotes   (139   quotes).   (n.d.).
Www.goodreads.com.
https://www.goodreads.com/quotes/tag/validation

Visualize   Quotes   (25   quotes).   (n.d.).
Www.goodreads.com.
https://www.goodreads.com/quotes/tag/visualize

Printed in Great Britain
by Amazon